RAIDING THE REICH

Mosquito B.16s of No 692 Squadron at Graveley, 20 October 1944. Each carrying a 4,000lb 'Cookie', Mosquitos of the Light Night Striking Force tormented many German cities throughout the winter of 1944–45. Losses were light, but the aircraft in the foreground, PF392/P3:R, never returned from Berlin on 21/22 March 1945. W Off I. M. MacPhee and Sgt A. V. Sullivan were the crew. The B.16 had bulged bomb-bay doors to accommodate the large bomb and also 'slipper' fuel tanks on each wing to extend range with this heavy load. (IWM CH17859)

RAIDING THE REICH

The Allied Strategic Offensive in Europe

ROGER A. FREEMAN

Caxton Editions

ARMS & ARMOUR PRESS
An imprint of the Cassell Group
Wellington House, 125 Strand. London WC2R 0BB

This Edition Published 2000 by Caxton Editions
an Imprint of the Caxton Publishing Group

British Library Cataloging-in-Publication data:
A catalogue record for this book is available from the British Library.

ISBN 1 84067 153X

Edited and designed by Roger Chesneau/DAG Publications Ltd

Printed at Star Standard Singapore

CONTENTS

Neutral countries
thus

Targets in Norway

Oslo
Stockholm
NORWAY
SWEDEN
DENMARK
Gdynia
Wilhelmshaven
Kiel
Anklam
8th AIR FORCE Base Area
Bremen
Berlin
G E R M A N Y
HOLLAND
Halberstadt
Bernburg
Merseburg
Hamm
Dresden
Antwerp
Gotha
Brux
BELGIUM
CZECHOSLOVAKIA
Lille
Schweinfurt
Méaulte
Regensburg
Paris
Stuttgart
Augsburg
Steyr
Lorient
Munich
AUSTRIA
St. Nazaire
F R A N C E
SWITZERLAND
Bordeaux
I T A L Y
Rome
Toulouse
15th AIR FORCE Base Area
750 miles radius of action B-17/B-24
PORTUGAL
S P A I N

Bases in Russia used for shuttle missions, June to October 1944

Bases in North Africa used for shuttles in 1943

PREFACE

The bloodiest and most extensive human conflicts occurred during the first half of the twentieth century. One, eventually known as the First World War, was centred chiefly on Europe; it was followed two decades later by truly global hostilities, justifying the title of the Second World War. The conflict in western Europe involved the same civilised people as the earlier war, following which the defeated nation had embraced an extreme dictatorial regime with military ambitions. Winning a war had now become as much a matter of superior technology as of the combatants' prowess: the war economy involved the whole nation as never before.

A new force in war was developing apace at this time—air power. During the Second World War the British Royal Air Force and the United States Army Air Forces undertook a campaign of aerial bombardment of Nazi Germany's war economy. It was a bloody business for both sides. The means of conducting this offensive and contesting it quickly become outdated and the battle is thus unique in history.

This book presents a selection of photographs taken during the bomber offensive for the record and for public information via the daily press. Scenes of actual battle were rare, particularly for RAF Bomber Command, which operated principally under cover of darkness. Non-official photography was limited by strict control of cameras and film, although a blind eye was turned to this by many servicemen, particularly Americans. Because of the limited number of official photographs covering specific actions and events, predominantly on the RAF side, several of the photographs here reproduced have appeared elsewhere. However, the wartime caption detail of these was sparse, in the cause of security, so research has been directed to discovering the who, when, where and why of the subjects depicted, in order to provide new interest.

A number of published works were used as references in the preparation of this volume and the reader is directed to the following for more detailed information on the bomber offensive. For the Royal Air Force the excellent *The Bomber Command War Diaries* by Martin Middlebrook and Chris Everitt is recommended for basic cover on the Command's operations for the whole war period. More technical detail and statistical in-

formation can be found in *Sir Arthur T. Harris: Despatch On War Operations,* published as a book by Frank Cass. The official *Strategic Air Offensive against Germany* by Sir C. Webster and N. Frankland provides a more penetrating study from the historian's viewpoint, as does John Terraine's *The Right Of The Line.* For individual units Philip Moyes' *Bomber Squadrons of the RAF and their Aircraft* is still unsurpassed as a comprehensive reference. More about bomber squadrons can be learned from the Air-Britain series of aircraft monographs, of which that on the Hampden, by Harry Moyle, must rate as one of the best service histories of an individual model yet published. For detailed information on the RAF's three main heavy bombers, the books by Michael Bowyer on the Stirling, Ken Merrick on the Halifax and Bruce Robertson on the Lancaster, and Francis K. Mason's more recent study of this last and most famous aircraft, are recommended. In addition, the pleasing evocations of all things Lancaster that are found in the *Lancaster at War* series by Mike Garbett and Brian Goulding must not be overlooked. Various documents were consulted at the Public Records Office and much of the caption detail is based on the individual squadron logs under AIR27.

For the United States Army Air Forces, references were the official Craven and Cate volumes, the USAAF Statistical Summary and a similar, more detailed publication for the Eighth Air Force. The *US Strategic Air Forces Weekly Digest* was also consulted. A reader requiring more information on Eighth Air Force operations should find this in the author's four *Mighty Eighth* volumes.

Additionally, considerable help and editorial advice was given by Bruce Robertson, a former editor of an Air Ministry journal and an acknowledged authority on the Royal Air Force and British warplanes in general, to whom the author wishes to express his sincere thanks. Acknowledgement is also made to Paul Kemp and the staff of the Imperial War Museum Photograph Archive for their courtesies; to Ian Mactaggart for additional photographic assistance; and to Russell Strong, Arlo Bartsch, George Birdsong and Mike Killaspy for information.

Roger A. Freeman
June 1996

1
ORIGINS

The invention of a heavier-than-air machine that allowed manned flight was not long in gaining the interest of the military, at first for aerial observation of an enemy's ground forces and, as the aeroplane was developed, for the carriage of armament and ordnance for defensive or belligerent purposes. The grenade, an encased explosive charge placed or projected by hand, was enlarged for dropping on an enemy as a bomb. The combination of aeroplane and missile offered an offensive capability far beyond artilllery range, opening a new era in warfare. The 1914–18 European conflict, which subsequently became known as the First World War, hastened aeronautical development apace. From harassing the area of the enemy's front, the aeroplane was soon capable of raids of fifty miles or more into an enemy's homeland. These intrusions rarely achieved any military advantage, but they did create a general unease among civilian populations that had hitherto been immune from actual hostilities.

Within a few weeks of the outbreak of war in 1914 the combatants were employing aircraft on organised bombing raids beyond the immediate battle area. These were of little significance until 1915, when the Germans brought particular disquiet to the British, who for centuries had relied on their island status for security, by using Zeppelins to drop bombs on London. This brought calls from both public and government for retaliation with attacks on major German cities, not immediately possible because the distances involved were beyond the range of British aircraft then available. In the course of endeavouring to meet this political demand, a concept evolved for a rapid development of aerial forces devoted to the interruption of the German industrial effort and, as the War Cabinet put it, 'kindred objects'. The latter can be presumed to cover enemy morale. The notion was that it might make a substantial contribution towards bringing about a demand for peace. Thus the strategic bombing campaign as a war-winning factor evolved. The foremost proponent of this idea was Major-General Hugh Trenchard, who, in June 1918, commanded the Independent Force with a brief to pursue a bombing cam-paign against the German munitions industry. This organisation, a Royal Air Force venture, was to be expanded to involve air units from other Allied nations, notably the United States. Handley Page O/400 bombers dropped bombs weighing up to 1,650lb on targets in Germany. This aircraft, in large-scale production in Britain at six plants, had a backing of American production when the war ended. The larger, four-engine Handley Page V/1500 was at that time entering service to reach Berlin.

The Royal Air Force, the world's first independent service committed to air operations, was subject to severe contraction in the early post-war years, with little favour forthcoming from government for the continued development of a strategic bombing capability. The British nation, like the other major combatants, reeled from the appalling casualties of the Western Front: involvement in another conflict of such magnitude was unthinkable to the population at large. Expenditure on military aviation was severely curtailed. Trenchard, becoming Chief of Air Staff, might opine that the main potential of the aeroplane was as an offensive rather than a defensive weapon, but such views were politically unsavoury to a nation that only wished to address peaceful matters. The RAF itself might have been disbanded as a separate service and its units parcelled out to naval and military administration. That it survived was largely due to Trenchard's proposal of air control, particularly in Iraq and the North-West Frontier of India, which proved practical and economic. Bringing recalcitrant tribes to heel, particularly those of hillmen who would plunder the plainsmen, could be better effected by threat and, if necessary, action to bomb villages, destroy crops and machine-gun herds than by military expeditions. Incursions into tribal lands on punitive forays meant marshalling a large body of infantry and artillery that would suffer casualties by sniping in the advance and a heavy toll on both sides in the final assault.

The post-war pruning of the United States Army Air Service was even more drastic. The first of its units did not enter combat until April 1918, a year after America became involved in the war, although thereafter the build-up moved ahead swiftly. With the end of hostilities, demobilisation was equally quick as the United Sates withdrew into a policy of national isolation. Despite the desire of several Air Service senior officers to see a separate service created much along the lines of the Royal Air Force, the US Army traditionalists prevailed in viewing aircraft as no more than a versatile weapon to be used in the service of the ground forces. Brigadier-General William Mitchell, one of the senior commanders of the United States Army Air Service in France during the war, was much influenced by Trenchard's views and his outspoken antagonism to the traditional military eventually led to his court martial. In spite of this cautioning, other American air officers continued to foster the concept of strategic bombing.

Economic depressions preoccupied most developed nations during the 1920s and 1930s, causing military appropriations to be severely limited. However, when the Germans embraced the Nazi Party and Hitler came to power in 1933 with a dictatorial government, neighbouring states were soon given to consider rearmament.

Western apprehension as to Hitler's intentions was fuelled by his promotion of Germany's war industry, not least aviation. The disclosure of the Luftwaffe and its potential gave impetus to Britain's rearmament, which was nonetheless tardy. However, in 1936 the Air Ministry reorganised the RAF units into Commands by function instead of by means of an area and location structure. Bomber Command, with headquarters established at Uxbridge on 14 July, became the senior RAF Command.

The new Command controlled four bomber-equipped groups, Nos 1 and 2 with mainly light bombers, No 3 with chiefly twin-engine types and No 4 composed of Auxiliary Air Force squadrons. The aircraft, largely biplanes, were for the most part obsolete in comparison with the all-metal monoplane bombers with which the Luftwaffe was being equipped. New designs were on their way: the Fairey Battle and Bristol Blenheim light bombers, the Handley Page Hampden and Vickers Wellington 'mediums' and the Whitley 'heavy' would all become available for service during 1937 and 1938 as the aircraft industry was rejuvenated. Even so, with most branches of the British aviation industry having hitherto been starved of investment, overall technical capability still lagged behind that of Germany.

The view that the bomber was the mainstay of independent air power and would always get through to its target still held sway in the Air Ministry hierarchy. With the German threat, from 1936 a series of offensive plans was prepared, most involving Bomber Command. Of the sixteen plans and supplements—known as Western Air Plans—the priorities were given to W.A.1, attacks on the German Air Force and its aerodromes;

W.A.4, military communications, rail, road and canal; and W.A.5, manufacturing resources, with special plans for the Ruhr and oil installations. The Ruhr, with its concentration of some 75 per cent of German solid fuel, steel and chemical production, became of prime interest, and studies were forthcoming on the numbers of bomber sorties necessary to incapacitate power plants and other crucial facilities. But all this was very much wishful thinking, for even with the new aircraft RAF Bomber Command was in no position to achieve the aims of these plans. A breath of realism was brought to the situation by Air Chief Marshal Sir Edgar Ludlow-Hewitt, soon after his appointment as Commander-in-Chief in the autumn of 1937. Generally acknowledged as one of the most talented and perceptive of RAF senior officers, Ludlow-Hewitt was soon to conclude that his new command was quite unprepared for war and only able to operate in fair weather. Piloting and maintenance standards were good, but navigation, bomb-aiming and gunnery were extremely poor. The predominant weakness lay in the ability to locate and attack targets, particularly in poor weather or darkness.

When the Second World War finally erupted with Hitler sending his forces into Poland on 1 September 1939, RAF Bomber Command had some 350 operational aircraft in 25 squadrons on home ground and ten squadrons with 160 Battles destined for the Advanced Air Striking Force in France (No 1 Group), while another eighteen home-based squadrons were in reserve status or acting as operational training units. Of their aircraft equipment, all types, other than the Wellington, were facing obsolescence, and the underpowered, single-engine Battle was already unfit for operational employment. Even so, the aircraft were generally reliable, which is more than can be said for much of the equipment and ordnance—most notably undependable radios, inadequate bomb sights and bombs of insufficient weight and ballistic efficiency. Many of these problems stemmed from a failure to identify and pursue shortcomings when concentration was primarily on expansion to match and overtake the Luftwaffe's strength. While the Luftwaffe's advantage in aircraft numbers was not as great as was thought at the outbreak of war, the German Air Force held the advantage in many technical matters.

Right: On the day Britain and France declared war on Germany following Adolf Hitler's invasion of Poland, Royal Air Force Bomber Command had a strength of 53 squadrons with a total of some 650 aircraft. The ten squadrons equipped with Fairey Battles of No 1 Group had flown to France the previous day and, of the remainder, eight were classified as reserve and non-operational while thirteen were engaged in operational training with No 6 Group. Of the five bomber types, the Vickers Wellington was to endure the longest in operational service, the first reaching the squadrons in October 1938. These are Wellington Mk Is of No 9 Squadron, flying near their Honington base a few weeks before the fateful 3 September 1939. None yet had power-operated gun turrets, and the aircraft would not go into battle until suitably modified. (IWM CH5)

2
BOMBER COMMAND
GOES TO WAR

few hours after Britain and France declared war on Germany, a Blenheim took off from the airfield at Wyton to conduct a reconnaissance of German naval ports. Britain, France and, eventually, Germany gave an undertaking not to attack targets where civilians might be harmed. In effect this meant that Bomber Command was limited to reconnaissance, attacks on naval vessels and the dropping of propaganda leaflets. That it was not immediately to be committed to any intensive bombing campaign gave further opportunity to address the many deficiencies in training and equipment. The ungainly Whitleys of No 4 Group, based in Yorkshire, had been considered suitable only for operations in dark-

ness from their introduction into service, and it was their crews to whom the task of delivering leaflets was given. The value of distributing millions of printed papers over major German cities was a contentious issue among RAF commanders. A confident nation, having achieved the defeat of Poland in three weeks, was unlikely to be swayed by enemy propaganda and did no more than profess annoyance at the untidy mess created in its streets, if German news media of the time are to be believed. The RAF men involved in these deliveries joked that they were suppling material that could be used for a more personal need by the recipients. However, an advantage that did accrue, during the six months that this activity preoccupied

Above and below: Leaflet operations, under the code-word Nickels, were the main operational activity of the Whitley squadrons during the first nine months of the war. It is known that many if not most of those aircraft missing during this period were victims of inclement winter weather. An example of what the elements could do is the sortie flown by Pilot Officer (P Off) Gray, captain of a five-man crew on No 102 Squadron Whitley serial number N1377, identity code letters DY:P, on the night of 27/28 November 1939. The crew had been briefed to drop leaflets on the port of Cuxhaven and carry out a reconnaissance of shipping in the area, and much cloud and extremely cold temperatures were encountered on the flight out. After the leaflets had been released from 15,000ft some four miles west of the target, Gray made a slow descent through cloud to carry out the rest of the mission. Ice formed on the aircraft and at 2,000ft snow was encountered. Although visibility was bad, the rear gunner reported seeing ships and Gray decided to make a second run. A searchlight briefly picked up the Whitley but did not hold. Soon afterwards there was a blinding flash which affected the front gunner's sight for a few minutes. Believing this to be anti-aircraft fire, Gray set course for Heligoland, climbing to 19,500ft before the accumulation of ice became so great that the aircraft became uncontrollable and dropped back through the clouds. Gray pulled the Whitley out at 2,500ft but as it was still unstable and difficult to control he gave instructions to prepare the dinghy for launching should the crew have to ditch. In preparation, P Off Long, the navigator, opening the fuselage door, saw that the upper surface of the port wing was stripped of fabric. The captain, finding that he could still control the aircraft, set course for home, flying at between 500 and 800ft to minimise ice formation. Fortunately three bearings were obtained from Bircham Newton before the wireless transmitter failed. Averaging an indicated air speed of 110mph, the aircraft made landfall at Great Yarmouth and a safe landing at Bircham Newton. The flash, thought to have been enemy fire, proved to have been a violent electrical storm which inflicted severe damage to the fabric on both wings. Approximately half the skin was missing from the top of the port wing for almost the entire span and about a third of that on the starboard wing was torn away. (IWM C48/C49)

Whitley squadrons, was the experience gained in night operations, particularly navigation. At the same time the crews returned with useful information by observations on the disposition of searchlights, anti-aircraft artillery, airfield illuminations and much that could be of value to intelligence. These sorties, rarely running into double figures for a single night, were often carried out in unfavourable conditions and the few losses sustained were mostly brought about by inclement winter weather.

The Blenheim, Hampden and Wellington squadrons were trained for daylight operations, but the first-named type did not have sufficient range for extended bombing operations along the north German coast. Most of the activity by these squadrons was conducted against German naval vessels when the opportunity allowed. The belief that flights of three bombers, with the new powered gun turrets, could successfully fight off enemy fighter interceptions was soon in question. Matters came to a head on 18 December 1939 when 24 Wellingtons from No 3 Group were despatched to attack German ships reported off Wilhelmshaven. Two aircraft turned back with

Above: For long-distance Nickel operations the Whitley squadrons used a forward base in France. On 30 November 1939 Flying Officer (Fg Off) G. E. Saddington and crew flew N1357/KN:H to Villeneuve to refuel and then carry out a sortie, returning directly to home base at Driffield. These sorties proved bitterly cold for crew members, particularly the rear gunner, who often wore a fur-lined apron. This Whitley was lost after a Nickel flight over the Ruhr on 28 March 1940 when Fg Off Geach and crew trespassed over neutral Holland and the bomber was shot down by a Dutch fighter. Sgt Miller was killed, the rest of the crew interned. (IWM C496)

mechanical trouble and the remaining 22 met both anti-aircraft fire and fighter interception in a near cloudless sky. Twelve of the Wellingtons were shot down—55 per cent of the force. As the bombers' gunners claimed an equal number of Me 109s shot down (the actual German losses numbered two) and critiques identified the lack of dorsal gun positions and self-sealing fuel tanks and poor formation flying as reasons for this high loss, there were those in the RAF who thought that, given improvements, the self-defending bomber might still hold its own.

Among senior commanders and authorities a more realistic appraisal concluded that continued operations in daylight were

Left, upper: The self-defending bomber concept was severely tested on 14 December 1939 when Bomber Command despatched a mixed force of more than forty medium and heavy bombers—the Whitley being classified as the heavy type—on armed shipping reconnaissance in the vicinity of German North Sea ports. The twelve Wellingtons involved were all from No 99 Squadron and led by the CO, Wing Commander (Wg Cdr) J. F.Griffiths in N2958. Take-off from Newmarket Heath was commenced at 1143hrs, each aircraft carrying three 500lb SAP (semi-armour piercing) bombs. An enemy convoy was sighted north of Wilhelmshaven but because of intermittent low cloud the formation was hindered in making an attack and became somewhat spread out while manoeuvring and avoiding anti-aircraft fire. Me 110 fighters then arrived on the scene and in the ensuing air battle five of the Wellingtons were shot down. Of the seven that escaped, one crashed while attempting to land at base. Five of the enemy fighters were claimed and one was admitted by the Germans. Despite the loss of half his force, Wg Cdr Griffiths maintained his faith in daylight operations, believing that this débâcle was due to particularly unfortunate circumstances. The events of four days later were to suggest otherwise. (IWM C246)

Left, lower: News media propaganda held the Fairy Battle to be a modern bomber well able to fend for itself. Front-line sorties during the 'Phoney War' period of winter 1939–40 soon suggested that the type was far too vulnerable to fighter interception. Battle K9330/MQ:W of No 226 Squadron, nicknamed *Tin Lizzie* by its regular crew, stands on snowy Rheims airfield in January 1940, one of some 150 Battles available in France. Few survived light flak and fighters during the German Blitzkrieg of May 1940. *Tin Lizzie* was not airworthy when the squadron was forced to abandon Rheims on 16 May and was set on fire and destroyed. (IWM C602)

Right, upper: No 18 Squadron, a Blenheim unit with No 6 (Training) Group at the outbreak of war, was sent to France to engage in strategic reconnaissance for the Air Component. Many operations were for the purpose of building intelligence files on Germany's war industry. Departing from the French base, these sorties, if successful, often terminated at a Bomber Command base in England. Squadron aircrew who distinguished themselves in these risky operations were, in late March

1940, assembled in front of a Blenheim for what had become the typical pose in all air forces. Left to right are Sgt A. C. Thomas, one of the most operationally active pilots in the unit; Sgt F. C. Miller; Flt Lt G. Wyatt; and Sgt G. Hawkins. Wyatt had just been awarded the DFC, the others the DFM. Hawkins distinguished himself on 31 October 1939 by aiding the success of a sortie despatched from Méharicourt to cover the Hamm–Hannover area, withdrawing over the North Sea to land at Watton. Sgt Thomas died of wounds received during an operation on 11 May 1940. Blehheim L6800/WV:Q appears to have flown only one combat sortie with No 18 before being transferred. It was written off in a landing accident at Upwood on 25 July the following year. (IWM C943)

likely to be at similar high cost—a loss rate which could not be sustained by Bomber Command. Thinking then centred on turning the Wellington and Hampden squadrons to night operations, for No 4 Group's Whitleys had already shown that this was the best way in the prevailing circumstances to evade the enemy's defences. While joining the Whitleys on leaflet sorties, the Wellingtons and Hampdens continued to operate against enemy shipping, but usually well removed from the German coastline and the attentions of intercepting fighters. The more nimble Blenheims of No 2 Group gradually became the main attack force against North Sea shipping within their range.

The first planned and executed night bombing operation by Bomber Command occurred on the night of 19 March 1940, when 30 Whitleys and 20 Hampdens were despatched to attack a seaplane station on the island of Sylt. This was a retaliatory raid for the Luftwaffe's attack on Scapa Flow a few nights earlier, when some bombs had fallen on land and killed a civilian. The cost was one Whitley. Although crews reported accurate bombing and much destruction, later photographic reconnaissance did not bear this out. The discrepancy between what crews believed they saw and what actually occurred was a situation that would persist in air actions to the end of the war, the result of a combination of speed, restricted outlook and charged adrenalin. Likewise, crews were often not where they believed they were during night sorties, as evidenced notably by trespass over neutral countries, particularly Holland.

On 9 April 1940 Hitler sent his forces into Denmark and Norway, a campaign completed within two months, despite attempts at intervention by Britain and France. Bomber Command was quickly committed with both day and night action against enemy shipping and airfields, with some tactical successes but generally having a negligible effect on the enemy's completion of his conquest. A new task was undertaken by Bomber Command on the night of 13/14 April when fifteen Hampdens of No 5 Group were despatched to drop mines in the sea lanes used by the Germans to reach Norwegian ports. One aircraft failed to return from this operation, the first of this nature that would become a regular duty for Bomber Command squadrons until the last days of the war.

Once more daylight forays encountering enemy fighter opposition brought heavy losses—yet more proof of the failure of the self-defending bomber concept. But the perils of operating bombers in daylight were even more clearly evidenced in the weeks following the launch of the Wehrmacht's offensive in the west on 10 May by invading Holland and Belgium. The majority of Bomber Command forces were immediately committed to attacking tactical targets, the Whitleys, Hampdens and Wellingtons operating by night while the Blenheims of No 2 Group flew by day. The Blenheims were placed under the tactical control of the RAF's Advanced Air Striking Force, to which No 1 Group's Battle squadrons in France were assigned, but operated from their East Anglian bases. In the course of the seven weeks it took the German forces to subjugate France a total of 97 were lost, nearly three-quarters of No 2 Group's authorised establishment, while the decimated Battle force returned to England minus some 140 aircraft, equivalent to the strength of almost nine of the ten squadrons. Significantly, when strong fighter support had been on hand, losses were often nil or much reduced.

France fell to what was then undeniably the most powerful military force on earth—the well trained, equipped and commanded Wehrmacht. The Luftwaffe had been created with a principal mission of supporting the ground forces, and this it did admirably. Its bombers were used tactically, and while this may be hard to equate with the attacks on areas of Rotterdam and other towns which do not appear to have had any direct military significance, the objective was to aid the progress of the ground forces. The bombing of Rotterdam was significant in that some of the barriers were removed on the restrictions for bombing in Germany proper. The implementation of the Western Air Plans had been British policy from the start of the German offensive, but this had been vetoed by the French, fearful of German retaliation: from their viewpoint, Paris was nearer to the enemy's airfields than was London. Britain bowed to the wishes of its ally.

From the first night of the German offensive, Bomber Command had been given dispensation to attack bridges and road and rail communications west of the Rhine under cover of darkness. Then, on the night of 15/16 May, 99 of a force of 111 Whitleys, Wellingtons and Hampdens despatched were briefed to strike targets in the Ruhr. While the main objective of these raids was to cause disruption that would affect the Wehrmacht's offensive, this action in effect marked the start of the strategic bombing campaign against Adolf Hitler's war effort.

Below: Two No 2 Group Blenheim squadrons were also sent to operate from France during the 'Phoney War' period. One was No 139 which, on 3 September 1939, had flown the first bomber Command sortie of the war. As with most of the RAF contingent in France, No 139 suffered heavy losses during the Blitzkrieg of May 1940. This Blenheim IV, N6227/XD:M, seen at Plivot in February 1940, was one that disappeared in the maelstrom, the exact date of its demise being lost with the squadron's destroyed documentation in France. Few of No 139's Blenheims survived; seven were lost out of nine attacking on 12 May. (IWM C1348)

Top: The six Whitley squadrons of No 4 Group were Nos 10 and 78 based at Dishforth, Nos 51 and 58 at Linton-on-Ouse and Nos 77 and 102 at Driffield. No other bomber squadrons operated the type, and when No 4 Group expanded it was with Wellingtons and finally Halifaxes. Described as 'a reliable old tub' by one Whitley cockpit veteran, it was classed as a night bomber from the outset. Photographed at Driffield during the first week of March 1940, these two Mk Vs of No 102 did not last long once the 'hot war' started in earnest. N1421/DY:C was lost to flak during an attack by six Whitleys on Fornebu airfield, Norway, on 29/30 April 1940; N1382/DY:A was shot down on an Augsburg raid, 16/17 August 1940. (IWM C921)

Above: A unique incident involving an RAF Bomber Command sortie occurred on the night of 15/16 March 1940. Flt Lt Tomlin and crew in Whitley N1387/KN:L of No 77

Squadron, having dropped leaflets in the vicinity of Warsaw, encountered bad weather during the return flight. Unable to find a French aerodrome in the first morning light, but seeing a large field, Tomlin decided that it was prudent to land before fuel reserves became too depleted. This was safely accomplished and members of the crew approached the local peasantry who had appeared. It was quickly established that they were not in France but Germany! A hasty return to the Whitley and a successful take-off was accomplished just as soldiers on cycles were observed approaching. The crew flew west, and a landing was made at the first French airfield encountered. N1387 came to grief after another long-range sortie, to bomb airfields at Trondheim in Norway on the night of 16/17 April 1940. Persistent cloud hindered the location of an airfield on return, and running out of fuel, the aircraft crash-landed at Grantown-on-Spey, Morayshire. (IWM C1007)

Right: Operating against the German forces that invaded Norway involved considerable distance and flights of long duration. A major requirement was knowledge of the disposition of the enemy forces, particularly in the northern areas, and Bomber Command was asked to help Coastal Command in this work. On 12 April 1940 Wellington L4387/LG:L, borrowed from No 215 Squadron and with extra fuel tanks in the bomb bay, was used by a crew from the recently formed No 75 (New Zealand) Squadron to carry out a reconnaissance north of Narvik. With a naval officer joining the crew, Flt Lt Breckon took off from Wick at 0800hrs and reached the vicinity of the Lofoten Islands at 1305hrs. A total overcast forced the reconnaissance to be made at between 500 and 800ft. Several photographs were taken and the only anxious moment was when a Ju 88 appeared. This did not intercept, however, and the Wellington returned safely to Wick 14 hours and 30 minutes after leaving—a record for an operational sortie that was not surpassed for some time. A total of 933 Imperial gallons of fuel were consumed, averaging 2.14mpg. The photograph shows Sgt Hughes, who navigated the trip, using his sextant. The fold-down seat is for the observer's use. (IWM CH67)

Below: The so-called Group Pool Squadrons of No 6 Training Group were mostly disbanded from 8 April 1940, having been used to form Operational Training Units. In the case of No 185 Squadron at Cottesmore, it simply changed its name on that date to No 14 OTU, finishing Hampden replacement crews for No 5 Group. This view from the top gunner's position shows Hampdens of this OTU while on formation practice. The narrow fuselage and its long bomb bay are well illustrated. The latter enabled the Hampden to carry a sea mine and, later, to be used as a torpedo bomber by Coastal Command. RAF Bomber Command eventually had 24 OTUs. (IWM CH715)

Above: The Handley Page Hampdens of No 5 Group began dropping magnetic sea mines in enemy waters in April 1940. The Hampden was the only aircraft which could encompass these weapons in its bomb bay at this time, and this task remained the aircraft's prerogative for some months, in addition to bombing operations. The Hampden had an unusual configuration which led to its sobriquet 'Panhandle'. Its performance was not impressive and it appeared to have an inherent problem related to loss of control, identified as 'stabilised yaw'. If crew positions were cramped, there was a good underfuselage defensive gun position. This formation of No 106 Squadron aircraft was photographed on 19 April 1940 when the unit was non-operational in a training capacity at Finningley. P1320/ZN:B was flown by P Off Page, L4182/ZN:K by P Off Hattersley and L4180/ZN:F by an unknown pilot as the Squadron Operational Record Book is in error by giving Page as the pilot of this aircraft too! Two of the aircraft were not long in meeting their ends after the squadron became operational in September 1940. L4180 went down in the sea near Spurn Head while returning from a raid on 29/30 October and P1320 spiralled into the ground north-west of Stamford on 25 November. (IWM HU69740)

Below: Stripped to the waist in the spring sunshine, armourers fuse a 250lb GP (general purpose) bomb before fitting it to the rack of a No 226 Squadron Battle at Rheims airfield. Despite valiant efforts and much bravery, the Battle squadrons could do little to check the Panzers and were decimated in a matter of days. The Battle's maximum bomb load was 1,000lb; within two years tactical fighters would carry such a load. (IWM C1689)

3
MUCH VENTURED, LITTLE GAINED

The priority objective for strategic attack was oil, primarily the synthetic plants in the Ruhr area which used lignite as the base material. Seventeen plants were identified, of which nine were estimated to be producing 80 per cent of the total output. Assessments of what was required to destroy or disable these were optimistic, and certainly unrealistic in view of the capabilities of Bomber Command. However, this priority would be reaffirmed in later directives, being based on the recognition of the dependency of modern armed forces upon petroleum products. The next priority targets for Bomber Command were communication systems, to hinder the movement of war materials, Luftwaffe airfields and aircraft factories, shipping, and port installations from which a cross-Channel invasion could be launched. This last-named task fell chiefly to the hard-pressed Blenheims of No 2 Group, which continued to suffer the heaviest losses of the Command as a result of their mainly daylight operations.

By the destruction of Germany's war potential through bombing, the effect it would have towards breaking the morale of the populace was being judged an important aspect, on which some authorities placed great score. With London and towns in the provinces reeling under attacks by the Luftwaffe, such direction would gain public support. However, in March 1941, with heavy losses of merchantmen to U-boats on the Atlantic trade routes, a directive changed priorities to the bombing of submarine bases and construction facilities. This remained in force for four months until an improvement in the Atlantic convoy situation permitted Bomber Command to return to its earlier priorities.

Despite Bomber Command's prowess being little different from that of September 1939 and its achievements doubtful, an extraordinary confidence persisted among its leaders that the objectives advocated could, in time, be achieved. Foremost amongst these men was the C-in-C, Air Marshal C. F. A

Left: A Royal New Zealand Air Force Flight had been established in No 3 Group at Feltwell in January 1940, manned largely by aircrew from that country. In April this was elevated to squadron status, becoming No 75 (New Zealand) Squadron, the first such Commonwealth unit in Bomber Command. Equipped with Wellingtons, its squadron code letters were 'AA' with 'Triple A' being used on most occasions by Sqn Ldr C. E. Kay, who became CO. While every aircraft had an individual serial number as a permanent identity, the five characters were too long for large-size display on the fuselage. The code letter system introduced shortly before the war provided a simple, highly visible means of identifying both an individual aircraft and its unit. Two adjacent letters provided the unit identity and a third letter that of the aircraft within that unit, this being separated, in most cases, from the unit letters by the fuselage roundel. The allocation of the unit codes was subject to security but, as many combinations remained unchanged throughout the war, the enemy became well aware of squadron identities. (IWM CH467)

Above: During the spring and summer of 1940 it was the Blenheims of No 2 Group which sustained the heaviest losses—nearly 6 per cent of sorties flown. Operating chiefly by day, they were used to support the withdrawal of British forces from France and then to harass ports where an invasion fleet might be assembled. In June their operations were extended to Germany with the intention of preventing the deployment of some Luftwaffe fighter units to the Channel coast. Maximum bomb load was 1,000lb for a 600-mile radius of action. No 110 Squadron's R3600 is here being armed with 250lb HE bombs and SBCs (small bomb containers) of 416 incendiaries at Wattisham in June 1940. Apparently it is being refuelled at the same time, ground crew attention is more numerous than usual and included is a squadron pet—all of which suggests a special display for the photographer. This aircraft survived until 6 May the following year when it was shot down while attacking a convoy. (IWM CH364)

Below: The Blenheim was about 100mph slower than its chief antagonist, the Messerschmitt Bf 109, and evasive action and cloud cover provided the best chance of survival for an aircraft if intercepted. The main defensive armament was two .303 calibre Brownings in the mid-upper turret, which were outranged by the fighter's cannon. To afford some defence against a low rear attack, Blenheim IVs were fitted with a .303 calibre K gun under the nose, sighted through mirrors and fired by the navigator/bomb-aimer. Later a controllable FN5A twin .303 Browning mounting was installed. This example of a K gun is fitted to R3874, a No 110 Squadron Blenheim at Wattisham in June 1940 which survived to serve in 13 OTU, eventually crashing shortly after take-off from Bicester. (IWM CH366)

Above: Whitleys of No 58 Squadron at Linton-on-Ouse under threatening clouds, summer 1940. P5028/GE:R outlasted most of her kind to be broken up in 1945. N1469/GE:H, usually flown by Flt Lt O'Neill's crew while at Linton, was later transferred to 19 OTU and flew into high ground near Arckiestown, Morayshire, during bad weather on 3 January 1943. No 58 had spent the winter of 1939–40 on detachment to assist Coastal Command in oceanic patrols before participating in Bomber Command's night bombing operations. As one of the last Whitley-equipped squadrons in No 4 Group, it did not convert to Halifaxes within the Command as did the others, for it was permanently transferred to Coastal Command in April 1942. The steel ringlet in the foreground is for tying down aircraft in high winds. (IWM CH222)

Below left: Installing the guns in the rear turret of a No 58 Squadron Whitley at Linton-on-Ouse. The four .303 calibre Browning machine guns delivered 80-plus bullets a second but the effective range was around 700yds and of little use against armour. Although numbers of enemy aircraft were shot down by these turret weapons, standard on all the main heavy bombers of the Command, the .303 machine gun was quickly rendered outclassed by the advances in German gun technology. (IWM CH246)

Above right: The Hampden had a maximum bomb load of 4,000lb. P1333/EA:F of No 49 Squadron is seen about to be loaded with six 250lb GP bombs at its Scampton dispersal. A few nights after this photograph was taken, on 16/17 August 1940, P1333 was one of two Hampdens that failed to return from an attempt to bomb the Merseburg oil plants. Flt Sgt M. Stetton and crew crash-landed in the Netherlands and were taken prisoner. Married quarters can be seen in the background, as can Hampden P1347/EA:D, which succumbed to flak on 4/5 September 1940 with the loss of all the crew. (IWM CH262)

Portal, who had taken over from Ludlow-Hewitt on 2 April 1940 (a normal planned command change) and remained until 5 October that year on becoming Chief of the Air Staff. Portal was a disciple of Trenchard, and no doubt his allegiance to the strategic bombing concept was reinforced by the generally buoyant mood of Bomber Command during his tenure.

The natural inclination of an armed service, striving to acquire strength, is to talk up its ability and achievements. In Bomber Command's case it was elevated by the crews' own genuine belief that their bombs had been placed on the target and that great destruction had been wrought. They felt that they were doing a good job. The night might hide the bombers but it also hid the truth, and the truth was hard to accept by the Command. The Germans had no intention of helping their adversary by revealing where bombs had struck, apart from the occasions when good propaganda value could be achieved. Even so, from analysis of such information as the enemy chose to give, plus reports from neutral countries, some disquieting conclusions should have been drawn. In spite of the firm evidence of bombing fifty miles or more from briefed targets, such errors were apparently dismissed as the occasional lapse rather than a frequent occurrence. More damning were the photographs from night cameras carried by some of the aircraft and the results of daylight photographic reconnaissance. Few bomb strikes could be plotted on many post-attack prints. There was occasional evidence of damage, and much was made of this in advancing the night bomber's case—even if its rarity was seemingly ignored.

In an effort to improve accuracy, major attacks were carried out in full-moon periods, with the hope of enabling crews to identify assigned targets visually. It remained extremely difficult, and individual crews could spend up to half an hour searching and still be unsure whether they had found the correct location. The Germans were quick to set up decoy fires, which undoubtedly tricked many bomber crews. While bright moonlight certainly improved the chances of finding the targets on cloudless nights, such were the exception, particularly in winter. More often the bomber crews had simply to rely on compass bearing and estimated time of arrival—dead reckoning—in the hope of arriving in the target area, where, if cloud, haze or other winter hazards held sway, bombing on target could only be a guessing game.

Despite the best endeavours of the crews, bombs were being strewn far and wide over western Germany during the first year of Bomber Command's attacks on that country. The weather also had a considerable bearing on the selection of targets and form of attack, resulting in a lack of concentration of effort against the priority targets over an extended period. The visual contrast between land and water at night was a consideration in target selection and led to the Dortmund–Ems Canal becoming very familiar to the British public through news communiqués. Waterways provided an important transportation system in the Ruhr area and the aqueducts carrying the canal appeared particularly vulnerable to bombing. However, this vital link remained obstinately resistant to the frequent attempts to sever it.

The difficulties of night bombing were clearly illustrated by what was happening on home ground at this time. Like Bomber Command, having found operations in daylight too costly, the Luftwaffe turned to the night for the protection for its bombers, proceeding to put London under sustained attack and dealing periodic heavy blows to other towns and cities during the winter of 1940–41 and the following spring. On many of these raids the Luftwaffe force was two or three times Bomber Command's maximum. Although the Luftwaffe was a tactical air force employed for strategic objectives during this campaign, its night operations were generally more advanced in execution than those of Bomber Command. The most significant advantage was the use of a specially trained unit to precede the main force in order to identify and mark the target with incendiaries and flares, having used a broadcast radio beam for accurate navigation. Notwithstanding these

Above: Blenheim IVs of No 40 Squadron taxying out at Wyton for a formation practice on 28 July 1940. Small stores racks under the rear fuselage were for smoke bombs. At the end of the year the Squadron converted to Wellingtons prior to its despatch to Malta, many of its aircraft and crews being transferred to No 114 Squadron. In this later service, on 13 January 1941, T1858 was sent under cover of cloud to conduct a reconnaissance of Nordhorn airfield, close to the German/Dutch border. It was the only Bomber Command aircraft on operations that day. It did not return. T1830/BL:Z, with crew aboard in this photograph, also went to No 114 and other service, surviving to be broken up as obsolete late in 1944. (IWM CH723)

Left: An observer—as the navigator/bomb aimer was known until March 1942—at his table in a No 40 Squadron Blenheim IV's nose. Restricted room did not allow standing upright but of more concern was a means of quick exit. The observer had to pass the pilot and use the roof hatch at the rear of the cockpit for egress. The bomb sight is the Mk II Course Setting Sight, which was standard equipment on Blenheims. (IWM CH752)

and other advantages, a considerable tonnage of the Luftwaffe's bombs was also dropped far from the assigned targets. There can have been few parishes in the south and east of England that did not receive a scattering of bombs during this period. Night bombing, despite its exponents' claims, was, then, of limited value where specific destruction was sought.

The Blitz on London brought retaliatory raids on the enemy's capital. Clouds hampered the attempt on 25/26 August 1940. While the British press made the most of this first attack on Berlin, it was ridiculed by the enemy's media, probably with justification as few bombs fell on the city. Still adhering to the brief to avoid unnecessary civilian casualties, the bomber crews were given specific targets. In the event it was, as usual, civilians who suffered most, albeit by default. The bombing of Mannheim on 16/17 December that year dispensed with any attempt to distinguish precise installations and for the first time a whole industrial town was the briefed target. Despite a full moon, good visibility and a small force of Wellingtons in the van to find and mark the city with incendiaries, German records showed a wide dispersal of bomb loads.

From the outset of hostilities Bomber Command acknowledged the difficulties of precise bombing in darkness, even if time was taken to appreciate the reality of the situation. An internal investigation in the spring of 1941 concluded that only 35 per cent of the bombers found the target and 50 per cent of loads were dropped in open country—an unpalatable report that apparently did not go beyond the Command. However, there were great hopes for a number of technical advances about to come into service. The most promising was a beam transmission to be used for precise navigation. The system, on which investigations had begun before the war and originally identified as G (later Gee), used two transmission stations whose signals were received by a device (the Gee Box) in an

Above left: On the night of 12/13 August 1940, Flt Lt Roderick Learoyd was the pilot of No 49 Squadron Hampden P4403/EA:M, one of eleven despatched from Scampton to make a low-level attack on the aqueducts carrying the Dortmund–Ems Canal over the River Ems near Münster. Previous Bomber Command attention to this vital transportation route into the Ruhr caused the Germans to place substantial flak defences along the approach line that any low flying aircraft would have to take in order to achieve accurate bomb strikes. In bright moonlight the Hampdens were clearly visible to the defenders, who shot down two and damaged several others. Learoyd's Hampden sustained severe damage during the target run at 150ft. The aircraft was repeatedly hit, large holes being blasted in the starboard wing. For a time Learoyd was blinded by searchlights and had to rely on his observer for guidance. When the aircraft returned to base, it was found that the hydraulic system had been hit and there was no control of flaps or undercarriage. Despite this, Learoyd put the aircraft down without injury to the crew. It was thought that his bombs caused a direct hit, for the damage was such that no water traffic could pass this point until repairs had been completed some ten days later. For his action that night Learoyd received the first Victoria Cross awarded for valour during a Bomber Command operation. There would be eighteen more. (IWM CH1004)

Above right: The Dortmund–Ems Canal breach achieved by Hampdens on 12/13 August, photographed on 21 September 1940 by a PR Spitfire. (IWM C2092)

aircraft. This enabled a navigator to obtain accurate positioning for up to 350 miles from source. The first operational trials, not conducted until the summer of 1941, were highly successful. Gee was then withdrawn for fear that one of the few sets might fall into enemy hands and be compromised before the aid could be brought into large-scale use. Another beam system, code-named Oboe, promised sufficient accuracy to become a dedicated bombing aid, although it too was of limited range, being dependent on ground stations. But the greatest interest was in a self-contained, ground-scanning, airborne radar set known as H2S. Both Oboe and H2S were in need of much development and were not available for operations until early 1942. Improved flares for target illumination were also in the offing, as was a more reliable bomb sight. The ordnance to effect greater destruction had been put in hand earlier,

2,000lb high-explosive bombs coming into use in July 1940 and the first 4,000lb blast bomb ushering in All Fool's Day 1941, courtesy of No 3 Group's Wellingtons.

The true operational strength of Bomber Command changed little during the first two years of war, for, although new squadrons were raised, others were being transferred to the Middle and Far East. Another factor was the poor rate of aircraft manufacture, particularly of the new heavy bombers whose design had been commenced way back in 1936. During that year the Air Ministry issued specifications for both four- and twin-engine bomber designs classified as heavy and medium-heavy. Contracts for prototypes were given to Short for the four-engine type and to Handley Page and Avro each for a twin featuring the promising Rolls-Royce Vulture of some 2,000hp. The Vulture was novel in being basically the mating of two

Left, upper: The next award of Britain's highest decoration for bravery also went to a Hampden crew member, and also to a Scampton-based airman. Sgt John Hannah was the wireless operator/air gunner on Hampden P1355/OL:W of No 83 Squadron, which took a direct hit from a small shell while attacking barge concentrations at Antwerp on 15/16 September 1940. A fire started in the rear of the crew compartment and burned fiercely. The under-gunner and the navigator thought the aircraft doomed and baled out. Sgt Hannah stayed to fight the fire and, having exhausted the extinguishers, beat out the remaining flames. The heat was so intense that ammunition exploded and metal was melted and

burnt through as shown in the photograph. His actions undoubtedly saved the aircraft, and P Off C. A.Connor was able to bring it safely back to England. (IWM CH1347)
Left, lower: John Hannah writing home while convalescing in hospital. In fighting the aircraft fire he was badly burned about the hands and face. At the age of eighteen Sgt Hannah was the youngest RAF recipient of the VC. (IWM CH1378)
Below: A Hampden of No 61 Squadron departs Hemswell at dusk on the evening of 15 October 1940. The target was Berlin, but as Berlin records no bombing for that night it may have been another instance of bombs discharged far from the target. (IWM HU69739)

existing engine designs into a single unit. Unhappily, the engine project was beset with continuing development troubles, so much so that in August 1937 the Air Ministry instructed Handley Page to redesign their bomber's wing to take four of the proven, if less powerful, Merlins. This was much against Handley Page's wishes, for it resulted in a virtual doubling of the design weight and brought attendant problems to the bomber—which would be named Halifax.

Shorts had considerable experience with four-engine flying boats and their design to some extent involved a substitution of the flying boat hull for a bomber fuselage. The restrictions of hangar dimensions and airfield landing grounds resulted in an aircraft wanting in wing area and with an angle of attack which put the aircraft's nose 15ft above the ground when at rest. The prototype Stirling did not fly until four months before the outbreak of war and the type's entry into operations was similarly tardy, not occurring until February 1941, and then on a limited scale. Failure of the ungainly undercarriage was the most serious of several mechanical and equipment problems, exacerbating an accident rate that production was initially hard pressed to replace.

By the end of 1941 there were still only three full Stirling squadrons and another forming. Of their total of 54 aircraft, an average of only 30 were serviceable for operations. Stirlings were often inhibited by the state of their No 3 Group airfields, where the sodden turf was not up to supporting the 25-ton monsters. The need for concrete runways had been recognised pre-war but the expense delayed implementation. The first sites to get them were the wettest, but, strangely, Fighter Command held priority.

The prototype Avro Manchester also flew a few weeks before the outbreak of war, production aircraft reaching the selected No 5 Group squadrons in November 1940 and these commencing operations in the following February. Throughout its development the Manchester was dogged with engine overheating and bearing failures, problems which continued in service. By the summer of 1940 Avro, suspecting that the Vulture's problems might never be satisfactorily overcome, set about installing a redesigned wing with four of the reliable Merlins, as had been done with the Halifax design at an early stage. The result was the Lancaster, first flown in January 1941. The Manchester had a sound airframe, and the superiority of the Lancaster configuration quickly led to the latter's substitution in production.

The Halifax prototype took to the air in October 1939 and the type was also subject to long delays before making its combat début in March 1941. Some 50 were in service with No 4 Group squadrons by the end of 1941. This aircraft, too, was not without its problems, notably a predilection for fatal stall spins. The cause was chiefly aerodynamic, taking many months to identify and correct.

Below: Stradishall was one of the immediate pre-war expansion period airfields built in East Anglia to house new bomber squadrons. Most had four C-type hangars, of brick and steel, well appointed with store and office annexes along their walls. During wartime aircraft were only taken into hangars for major repairs and, once these were completed, quickly removed. Hangars were a prime target for enemy hit-and-run raiders. Wellington T2470/BU:K, of No 214 Squadron, here being towed in for repairs during October 1940, was a victim of accident about a month later when, on Guy Fawkes Day, it crashed at Denston having overshot Stradishall. (IWM CH1415)

Left: In far from favourable weather, 77 Bomber Command aircraft were despatched on 12/13 November 1940 to harass a number of targets in the Ruhr, No 102 Squadron seeking an oil refinery at Wesseling. The crew of Whitley P5005/DY:N had some confusion in finding the target and after twenty minutes' searching the captain decided that they should bomb Cologne's marshalling yards instead. While investigating beneath the clouds, two direct hits were taken from light flak. One burst in the fuselage, detonating a flare and opening up a 15ft section of the port side as neatly as a can opener. Wireless operator Sgt. A. Davidson sustained slight wounds and the interior of the Whitley was temporarily filled with acrid fumes, the captain momentarily losing control and only managing to regain it after the aircraft had lost some 2,000ft in a dive. Despite the adverse aerodynamic effect of the flapping fuselage skin, the pilot was able to return safely to base. His name was P Off G. L. Cheshire and the feat brought him a Distinguished Service Order (DSO). Leonard Cheshire was destined to become one of the most eminent pilots to serve with Bomber Command. The dislodged flare that ignited can be seen below the hole in the far side of the fuselage; other flares are in the rack on the right. (IWM CH1765)

The workhorse of Bomber Command remained the Vickers Wellington, whose numbers had been built up to 280 by the end of 1941, near half the average serviceable force. No 1 Group's squadrons, whose Battles had been decimated during the Battle of France, moved from the Salisbury Plain district to re-form in the Nottingham–North Lincolnshire area, between the Whitley stations of No 4 Group and the Hampden airfields of No 5 Group.

During 1941 the Blenheims of No 2 Group continued to put their main effort into low-altitude daylight attacks on shipping and ports within their range, and on occasions suffered heavy casualties. By the autumn these activities were no longer deemed to be worth the results achieved, despite the fact that there had been successful bombings with vessels sunk or badly damaged. Following this reduction in offensive activity some Blenheim squadrons were converted to medium types and others sent overseas, while the remainder began conversion to the American-made Douglas Boston, a faster and more nimble light bomber . The Group was also host to an interesting operational experiment in daylight bombing during the summer of 1941.

The United States Army may have regulated bomber aircraft to serve the ground forces and appropriations for new aircraft of any type had been scant during the inter-war years, but fortunately a reasonably generous attitude prevailed in respect of the experimental and development work at Wright

Below: The first operation in which the Avro Manchester participated was the night raid of 24/25 February 1941, to bomb a *Hipper* class cruiser reported in Brest. Six aircraft of No 207 Squadron were involved, including L7284/EM:D with Fg Off P. R. Burton-Gyles and crew. One aircraft had undercarriage failure and crashed on landing back at Waddington. The Manchester had the highest combat loss-to-sorties ratio and the highest accident rate of all Bomber Command bomber types. This was due primarily to the persistent overheating and failure of the Vulture engines, troubles that were never satisfactorily overcome. With the loss of one engine the power from the other usually proved insufficient for flight to be maintained for long. With much-troubled engines, L7284 was removed from operational use in April 1941 and scrapped two years later. (IWM CH17297)

Field, Dayton, Ohio. This establishment was particularly successful in developing advanced equipment to aid high-altitude flight. Despite the depression years there was sufficient wealth in the USA to promote civil aviation and in particular air transport. The use of commercial airlines was gaining increasing popularity for shortening the time taken to travel from major cities hundreds of miles apart. In the design and construction of aircraft to meet this market, US manufacturers were in the forefront by the mid-1930s. These advances in airframe and engine design were also applicable to military aircraft, so that, when the enlightened Roosevelt administration recognised that sooner or later America would become embroiled in the defence of democracy and decided to increase funds for its armed services, the indigenous aircraft industry could respond with some excellent products.

The Boeing Model 299 of 1935 was the world's first all-metal monoplane bomber and a small batch was ordered by the US Army for extended trials. The Army Air Corps saw its

Left: Most air crews considered the interior of the Manchester's fuselage far better than that of the Halifax and Stirling. The Lancaster fuselage was basically the same as the Manchester's. This view of the cockpit of Manchester L7288/EM:H shows the dual controls and fold-down seat used by the flight engineer (an aircrew category introduced in March 1941) during take-off and landing. However, both Manchester and Lancaster found little favour with pilots in a bale-out emergency. Escape via the hatch in the cockpit 'roof' carried a risk of being swept into the mid-upper turret or tailfins, while the small nose hatch was a long way forward. Despite being the thirteenth production Manchester, L7288 endured through operational service and training until scrapped in May 1943. (IWM CH3880)

Below: Some RAF squadrons were given named associations with Commonwealth and Empire countries, in recognition of funds raised towards the 'purchase' of an aircraft for 'their' squadron. No 102 was the Ceylon squadron and T4261/DY:S, seen here in the snow at Topcliffe, was recognised as the Whitley which had been contributed by Ceylon. Unhappily, it did not endure for long, failing to return from Cologne on the night of 1/2 March 1941. (IWM CH2052)

potential as a vehicle for strategic bombing, and during the closing years of the decade, when Government and Army resistance to aircraft use for offensive purposes gradually faded, the B-17 (as the Boeing was designated in USAAC service) was used to advance a doctrine of daylight, high-altitude bombing. With an advanced crew oxygen system, turbo-supercharged engines and an amazingly accurate bomb sight, the B-17 could operate at heights of 25,000ft for prolonged periods.

The British and French governments had invested in US aircraft production in the late 1930s and, once isolated, Britain welcomed the most modern aircraft that America could supply. The USAAC's pride was the B-17, and in 1940 twenty of these bombers were offered to the RAF. Both Churchill and Roosevelt saw political capital in the B-17's use in bomber operations against Germany, whereas neither the RAF nor the USAAC were enthusiastic. The former did not consider that the B-17 lived up to its popular name, Flying Fortress, having no power-operated gun turrets, and so would be even more vulnerable to fighter attack than the British bombers. The USAAC was also aware of the bomber's deficiencies and did not want a precipitous combat commitment to bring disquieting reports which might jeopardise recently hard-won procurement of heavy bomber production. However, the twenty Fortresses were sent to the United Kingdom and a special RAF squadron was formed and trained to operate them.

Bomber Command believed that the only way the Fortresses could endure in daylight operations was if they operated above 32,000ft, where enemy interceptors would have difficulty in reaching them. In a series of raids, all by single aircraft or very small numbers, during the second half of 1941, RAF crews

Left, upper: Little publicity was given to individual RAF airmen in the early war years unless they were the recipients of a major award. An exception was Wg Cdr Percy Pickard DSO DFC, who was the pilot in the popular 1941 documentary *Target for Tonight*. This film featured the crew of Wellington 'F for Freddie', No 149 Squadron's P2517, in a flag-waving episode of the stiff-upper-lip genre. However, Pickard was a very distinguished pilot and leader. When this photograph was taken he was commanding No 51 Squadron, a Whitley unit at Dishforth, which he led to drop paratroops in a daring raid to capture a radar installation on the French coast at Bruneval. He lost his life while leading a Mosquito raid on Amiens prison in 1944 in an attempt to give freedom to French Resistance members incarcerated within. (IWM CH2185)

Left, lower: On the last night of March 1941, Bomber Command

introduced what would become a major weapon in its campaign against German industrial towns and cities, the 4,000lb HC (high capacity) blast bomb, which became known to RAF personnel as a 'Cookie' and to the British press as the 'Blockbuster'. One was delivered by Sqn Ldr K. Wasse in No 9 Squadron Wellington R1513 on Emden, the other to the same target by P Off Franks in No 149 Squadron's W5439/OJ:X, a Wellington Mk II, which had Merlin engines developing more power than the Mk I's radials. Both aircraft had their bomb bays specially modified to take these large missiles. The night camera of the No 149 Wellington took this view of the attack. One bomb destroyed 30 houses and caused devestation over a wide area, while the other obliterated the town's telephone exchange, telegraph and post offices. (IWM C1888)

Left: Luftwaffe night fighters, mostly twin-engine Me 110s and Ju 88s operating under ground control, were having some success against the bombers, particularly on moonlit nights. Of 99 bombers out on 9/10 April, most of the eight lost are believed to have fallen to fighter interception. One fortunate to escape was this No 99 Squadron Wellington, T2739, which was raked with cannon-fire near Berlin and lost the top of its fin and rudder. Flt Lt Harvey, here examining the damage, was able to bring the bomber back to make a safe landing at Waterbeach. Repaired, T2739 went on to serve with two other operational squadrons before retirement. The white cross on red panel marks where the fire extinguisher was originally stored. (IWM CH2513)

endeavoured to bomb from such high altitudes—with limited success. While there was little trouble from enemy fighters above 30,000ft, the Fortresses had great difficulty in maintaining these altitudes due generally to the strain of low temperatures on components. The experiment was terminated in September 1941. Nevertheless, with new-model Fortresses scheduled to reach the UK during the winter and the more promising four-engine Liberator bomber starting to arrive, Bomber Command formed a new group, No 8, to operate the American 'heavies' from new airfields in the Huntingdon–Northampton area. Its existence was brief, for, following the United States' entry into hostilities in December, few of its heavy bombers were forthcoming for the RAF and No 8 Group was disbanded.

From the spring of 1941 Bomber Command's strength increased from an average 150 serviceable aircraft to some 350 by the end of the year. But in the same period losses on night operations had risen from some 2 per cent of sorties to 3.5 per cent. If the bombing brought little hurt to the German war effort, its frequency was a portent of things to come and the Luftwaffe was now making determined strides to counter the night raids. A chain of radar detection sites had been set up from Norway down to south-west France, while a system of ground control interception areas was established whereby night fighters could be directed to the raiders. During full-moon periods the night fighters were becoming adept at finding the bombers, particularly those orbiting, trying to locate a target. Searchlight coordination with both fighters and anti-

aircraft artillery had also improved. Luftwaffe long-range fighters occasionally intruded over the bombers' home ground to shoot them down, the first such victim being a Whitley brought down in Yorkshire in October 1940.

However, the enemy was not the only cause of losses. Accidents took a toll, the exact degree unknown, but it was suspected that in poor winter weather several of the bombers that failed to return were the victims of mishap. There is little doubt that bad weather contributed to the Command's heaviest loss so far when, of 392 aircraft despatched on the night of 7/8 November 1941 to Berlin, Cologne and Mannheim, 37 failed to return—9.4 per cent of total sorties. The operation was given the go-ahead even though weather deterioration was forecast with heavy icing and storm cloud. This and other apparent lapses in direction were advanced as figuring in the removal of Bomber Command's chief, Air Marshal Sir Richard Peirse, in the following January. There were misgivings among senior Bomber Command and Air Ministry officers about the increasing casualties, particularly as an independent investigation of bombing results using reconnaissance photographs found that only one-third of aircraft claiming to reach the target actually dropped within a five-mile radius. Nevertheless, despite these concerns, in the situation existing a massive bomber offensive remained Britain's only foreseeable means of taking the war to the enemy. Apart from the immediate objectives, the campaign might help to take some of the pressure off the USSR, which had been attacked by Hitler's forces in June. The extensive bomber production and crew training programmes remained in place, even if the summer 1941 plan for 4,000 heavy bombers in 250 squadrons appeared over-ambitious.

Then, a few days after the Japanese attack on Pearl Harbor on 7 December 1941, Hitler and Mussolini unwisely declared war on the United States. America was already preparing for war and now agreed with Britain that Germany was the most dangerous of their adversaries and should be defeated first. To achieve victory, Allied armies would have to invade continental Europe, but until they were ready the US Army Air Forces (raised to that status from the Army Air Corps on 20 June 1941) would send units to join Bomber Command in its strategic campaign.

Left, upper: A full moon and a raid tonight: a panorama of the Wellington dispersal at Feltwell, home of No 75 Squadron from April 1940 to August 1942. The wartime caption states that these men are going out to their bombers, but the incomplete flying kit and the orderly line of ground crew personnel suggests that this stroll was set up for the photographer. Although most key airmen were New Zealand nationals, crews were frequently made up with men from Britain and other Commonwealth countries. Several of these smiling faces would soon be gone, for by the end of the war nearly a thousand members of No 75 were either dead or had been taken prisoner—one of the highest casualty rates in Bomber Command. (IWM CH2671)

Left, lower: Those who flew in *Firefly* were fortunate, for it did not burn in some foreign field as did many of the 1,386 Wellingtons lost in Bomber Command service. Aircraft R1593/OJ:N of No 149 Squadron would go on to serve with Nos 15 and 21 OTUs until no longer airworthy. This photograph was taken in about April 1941 at Mildenhall. The bombs are 250lb HE. Bombs were colour-coded yellow (as shown), red and green, for high-explosive, incendiary and smoke respectively. The later large HC bombs were green for camouflage. Bombs were further colour-coded: those shown have a red ring three inches from the nose, indicating that the case is filled, while a green band around the bomb further back indicates that the filling is high explosive. (IWM CH2705)

Right, top: On 6 June 1941 Winston Churchill visited West Raynham to review the RAF's latest bombers. The first squadrons equipped provided a Stirling and a Halifax, and a recently received Boeing Fortress was also displayed. Wg Cdr R. W. P. Collings, CO of No 35 Squadron, demonstrated Halifax L9506/TL:X for the Prime Minister. Ten nights later L9506 was shot up by a night fighter over Hanover and struggled back to crash-land at Bircham Newton. (IWM H10315)

Below right: The first Halifax squadron was No 35, based at Linton-on-Ouse. Here one of its early crews enjoys June sunshine by the technical site. They are, left to right, Sgt 'Revs' Brown, Sgt 'Taffy' Roberts, Sgt Hares (extreme top), Sgt 'Jacko' Jackson, Sgt Weldon, Fg Off 'Skip' Cheshire DFC and Sgt Gutteridge (centre bottom). They are believed to be the first Halifax crew to bomb Berlin, and their captain would become the most noted of all RAF Bomber Command pilots. (IWM CH6372)

Bottom right: The Blenheim was a popular aircraft with pilots, having few vices. As with all aircraft of its day, a loss of hydraulic pressure would often result in a forced 'belly landing', as befell No 21 Squadron's Z7432/YH:J on 6 July 1941. The fire crews at Watton were soon upon the scene and liberally doused the smoking Mercury engines with foam flame-suppressant. (S. Clay 1)

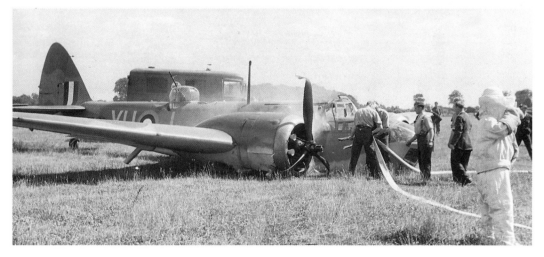

Left, upper: On the night of 7/8 July 1941 No 75 Squadron Wellington L7818 was flying over the Zuider Zee after attacking Münster when it was shot up from below by an Me 110. Cannon shell strikes (A) on the starboard wing caused a fire and feed from a fractured fuel line threatened to spread to the whole wing. After the crew had made strenuous efforts to douse the flames with extinguishers through a hole in the fuselage, the captain, Sqn Ldr R. P. Widdowson, alerted the crew to be prepared to abandon the aircraft. The second pilot, Sgt James Ward, volunteered to go out through the astro-hatch (B) to try and put out the flames. With a rope tied round his waist he managed to make holes (1, 2, 3) in the fabric and moved down the fuselage side and out across the wing. Miraculously, he was not swept off by the propeller slipstream and managed to smother the fire in the wing fabric. Exhausted, he regained the aircraft. With no adjacent fabric to burn, the engine fire gradually faded. Sgt Ward was awarded a VC for his extraordinary action, but, sadly, he was to perish on the night of 15/16 September when the Wellington in which he was flying was shot down over Hamburg. Wellington L7818, in which the award was gained, was sent to 15 OTU after repair. On 8 April 1942 it collided with a Spitfire in a rainstorm and crashed at Cold Ashton, Gloucestershire. (IWM CH3223)

Left, lower: An added purpose of Bomber Command's daylight operations was to keep a good proportion of the Luftwaffe's day fighters in the west, thus giving some aid to the USSR which was invaded by the Wehrmacht in June 1941. To attain surprise, low-level approach was carried out by Blenheims against heavily defended targets. This was to little avail at ports such as Bremen, bristling with both light and heavy flak weapons. When twelve Blenheims were sent to this target on 4 July they had the misfortune to pass a German vessel before making landfall. Wg Cdr Hughie Edwards, CO of No 105 Squadron and leading, knew there was a likelihood that the ships' crew would radio a warning to a shore base, but he decided to press on with the attack. The barrage that met the bombers brought down a third of their number and damaged all the remainder to some degree. Edwards received a VC for his leadership that day. It is believed that Edwards' turret gunner took this photograph of bomb explosions from V6028/GB:V as it sped away at 50ft—the lower one flew the less time the flak gunners were given to correct aim. (IWM C2094)

Right, top: Luftwaffe officers examine the wreck of V6020/OM:W of No 107 Squadron, one of two Blenheims claimed by the 8th (Motorised) Flak Division during the attack on Bremen, 4 July 1941. Brought down at Blockland at 0806hrs, the Blenheim is believed to be that flown by Flt Lt Wellburn. (IWM HU25727)

Right, centre: Some of the low-level photographs brought home by Blenheims were spectacular. On 16 July 1941 36 aircraft bombed the shipping in Rotterdam docks, damaging at least twenty vessels. Flak brought down four of the attackers, including V6267/WV:M of No 18 Squadron shortly after this photograph was taken. Flown by the squadron CO, Wg Cdr Partridge, the Blenheim was seen to crash in a river. Partridge had only joined the squadron at the beginning of the month, bringing his observer, Sgt Dvorjetz, with him. (IWM C1951)

Bottom: A flight of three No 21 Squadron Blenheims dashes over the Dutch countryside on the approach to Rotterdam docks, 16 July 1941. The squadron was lucky to have no losses that day, but the fortunes of war were such that the nearest aircraft, V5595/YH:P, with Flt Sgt Kemp's crew, was lost on its next operation, a shipping strike, two days later. (IWM C1953)

Above: Winston Churchill with a party of foreign guests and officials, including senior US officers, during an inspection laid on at Northolt, 21 July 1941. Following Churchill is the Secretary of State for Air, Sir Archibald Sinclair, always a dapper dresser. The bombers displayed included a prototype Lancaster, a recently arrived Fortress I, Halifax L9503/TL:P of No 35 Squadron and Stirling N6003/MG:V of No 7 Squadron in the foreground. (IWM CH17535)

Below: A No 90 Squadron Fortress I takes off from Polebrook on 24 July 1941, destination Brest. Three of the squadron's aircraft were sent to attack the battlecruiser **Gneisenau** from 30,000ft, to draw enemy fighters to intercept, allowing, it was hoped, less attention to a large force of Hampdens and Wellingtons bound for the same target. The enemy vessel was hit by a number of bombs at the cost of a dozen of the attacking force, although the Fortresses returned unscathed. Operating six miles above the earth may have offered some immunity, but the strain on the Wright engines was such that this altitude was difficult to sustain. The Sperry Model O bomb sight also failed to provide the necessary accuracy in attacks from such great heights. Although Polebrook has a J-Type (curved roof) and a T-Type hangar at this date, airfield construction is still in progress. (IWM CH3086)

Right, top: On an afternoon in the second week of August 1941, Halifax Mk I L9530/MP:L ambles among the clouds near its Middleton St George base. When possible, it was policy to assign a crew to the same aircraft, as this bestowed confidence. Flt Lt Christopher Cheshire captained the men of L9530, their luck running out on the bomber's next operation, its fifth, on 12/13 August, when it was one of two from No 76 Squadron that failed to return from Berlin. Flt Lt Cheshire survived as a prisoner of war (POW). A year later to the day his brother, Sqn Ldr Leonard Cheshire, flew his first sortie as the new CO of No 76, a position he would hold for a year. (IWM CH3389)

Right, centre: The RAF's first four-engine heavy bomber, the Short Stirling, was hampered by numerous technical troubles from its first squadron assignment in August 1940, delaying the commencement of night operations until the following February, and then on a limited scale. For a period in July 1941 the Stirlings were involved in Circus operations, the use of a small number of bombers to provoke a response from Luftwaffe fighters which the large RAF escort would counter. On 5 July Flt Lt Gilmour was the captain of N3658/LS:E in company with two other No 15 Squadron Stirlings sent to bomb a factory at Lille. On penetrating enemy airspace at 10,000ft, the crews encountered intense and accurate flak, fortunately with no direct hits. Perforations were sustained but N3658 returned safely to base, as did the rest of the trio. On other similar intrusions Stirlings did fall victims to flak and it was eventually decided that these large bombers were too vulnerable at their operational altitude for this type of raid. (IWM C2029)

Right, bottom: Having lost three sons in RAF service, Lady MacRobert furnished the cost of a Stirling to be named in their honour as *MacRobert's Reply*. Wg Cdr Pat Ogilvie DSO, No 15 Squadron's CO, is seen here presenting a 'good luck' letter to the crew, captained at this time by Fg Off Peter Boggis, who would normally fly this aircraft. *MacRobert's Reply*, N6086/LS:F, seen in the background, flew twelve sorties and after major maintenance was used by No 1651 Heavy Conversion Unit (HCU) at Waterbeach. It crashed in Oakington village on 14 March 1943 after losing a wing. (IWM CH3945)

Left, top: Two power stations near Cologne were identified as supplying much of the needs of war industry in the region and an elaborate plan to attack them was devised. On 12 August 1941 54 Blenheims were despatched on a low-level raid which would take them well beyond the range of friendly fighter support. The major target was at Knapsack, $7^1/2$ miles south-west of Cologne, to which 38 Blenheims were sent. They were met by intense anti-aircraft fire. The No 114 Squadron aircraft in the photograph, V6391/RT:V, with Sgts Broom, North and Harrison as pilot, observer and air gunner respectively, survived the flak; the crew would be sent to the Middle East a month later and V6391 would survive until lost in an intruder operation over Holland the following January. (IWM C2025)

Left, centre: Two 500lb bombs from a Blenheim explode near the coal-handling plant at the Fortuna power station near Cologne, 12 August 1941, photographed from the turret of an aircraft flying at less than 100ft. Flak bursts are discernible in the distance. (IWM C2024)

Left, bottom: While over the Zuider Zee, returning from operations on the night of 12/13 August 1941, No 75 Squadron Wellington X9764/AA:V was hit by a long burst of fire from a night fighter. The enemy aircraft did not attack again, but damage to the Wellington was extensive. By the time the vicinity of the home base at Feltwell was reached, fuel was nearly exhausted. Roberts ordered the other five crew members to bale out but he had no time to leave his seat and jump before the engines cut out. In the bright moonlight Roberts saw that he was going to crash among the young conifers of Thetford forest but fortunately he was able to guide the aircraft into one of the wide firebreaks. Wellingtons were highly repairable and, despite the damage, X9764 was back in service a few months later, only to be lost with a Polish crew of No 304 Squadron in the Cologne raid of 5/6 April 1942. (IWM CH3366)

Above: The Standard Fordson farm tractor, basically a First World War design, served as a tug for bomb 'dollies' and aircraft on many Bomber Command airfields. The RAF version was provided with better brakes than the farm tractor and ran on petrol rather than vaporising oil (kerosene). It needed full power and low gear to move 15 tons of Halifax. This one is shifting a mud-spattered No 10 Squadron Halifax, L9621/ZA:P, at Leeming in January 1942, an aircraft that was retired from operations only to be wrecked in a bad-weather landing accident at Croft in the following spring. (IWM:CH4459)

Right: Thousand-pounders fall from the wing racks of a Wg Cdr B. V. Robinson's Halifax during the attack on the German warships in Brest harbour, 18 December 1941. The No 35 Squadron CO was flying V9978/ TL:A, and while leaving the target the aircraft's port inner engine was hit by flak. A fire started and soon spread to the other port engine. Although the fires were eventually extinguished, the aircraft lost height and the Wing Commander decided to ditch in the sea. This was accomplished successfully some 60 miles from England and all members of the crew were rescued, little the worse for their experience. (IWM C3046)

4
TURNING POINTS

February 1942 witnessed notable events in the fortunes of the bombing offensive. On the 24th the Air Ministry issued a directive which required Bomber Command to 'focus attacks on the morale of the enemy civil population, and, in particular, of the industrial workers'. For the first time the destruction of cities and towns rather than of the industries they contained had become the primary objective. In effect this was an admission that two years of night operations had not produced any significant hurt to the German war economy because so few bombs had found their specified targets. If Bomber Command could not hit the factories, it would have to kill the people who worked in them and disrupt urban life to such an extent as to cause a breakdown in morale. Thus was 'area bombing' approved, although any major attack upon an industrial conurbation would also chance to bring some destruction to factories and other war-supporting installations.

The breaking of the enemy civilian populace's morale had long been nurtured in some quarters as an attainable result of a massive bombing campaign, unpalatable as it was on humanitarian grounds. Ideally, the bombers' objectives were oil, munitions and specific targets which would harm the enemy's war economy, but these goals proved beyond the current resources of the Command. The Luftwaffe's apparent disregard of civilian casualties in bombing British towns and cities had mellowed objections to bringing similar slaughter to German communities. What had come about in this total war was the fading of any distinction between the military and the civilians who supported it. The news media of the combatant nations were contemptuous of the enemy in the cause of boosting morale, but it is surprising that the Air Ministry planners followed a similar line by believing the Germans inferior in courage and resilience. London had undergone some 72 nights of continuous bombardment during the 1940–41 winter and, if anything, Londoners' morale had strengthened.

The directive was approved by Portal, if its content was framed by others who could see no other path to take in the existing situation. While the new chief of Bomber Command,

Above: Adornment of aircraft with personal motifs and insignia was tolerated in the cause of morale. One suspects that this reflection on a well-known saying of the film star Greta Garbo was thought appropriate for the lone night sorties undertaken by the crew of a No 218 Squadron Wellington at Marham. At this time, late 1941, the squadron was about to exchange its Wellingtons for Stirlings. (IWM CH3424)

Air Marshal Arthur T. Harris, appointed on 22 February, had no qualms about pursuing the new primary objective, it was most certainly not at his instigation, notwithstanding popular opinion in years to come. In his fiftieth year Harris had commanded No 5 Group for twelve months at the beginning of the war and was known for a lively mind and resolute disposition, if veering towards dogmatism on some matters. Above all, he had that most vital asset of a successful commander—an unrelenting determination to succeed.

On the previous afternoon, another officer who would play a prominent part in the bombing offensive first arrived on the scene. Brigadier-General Ira Eaker was sent by General H. H. Arnold, head of the USAAF, to understudy RAF Bomber Command and to set up a headquarters for a similar organisation to control American bomber units that would follow. Although committed to the strategic bombing concept, Eaker had spent much of his recent service with fighter organisations, and his selection by Arnold for the task in Britain was in part due to

Eaker's noted diplomacy. Arnold appreciated that, as the newcomer, the USAAF would initially depend heavily on the RAF for both guidance and material assistance, but at the same time the American force would be pursuing a method of operation that the British considered unlikely to succeed.

Despite the abandonment of large-scale daylight bomber operations by both RAF Bomber Command and the Luftwaffe, the USAAF had continued to pursue the development of its high-altitude, daylight precision bombing doctrine. Redesigning the B-17 had resulted in power turrets being added and up to a dozen machine guns in seven positions. The newer B-24 Liberator was similarly equipped. Their machine guns were not the rifle-calibre (.300/.303in) weapons as in British bombers but of .50in calibre, having a higher muzzle velocity and giving great destructive power and, most advantageously, an effective range over three times that of the .303. By flying a dozen so of these bombers in tight formation, any intercepting fighters, it was believed, could be driven off. While flying in the sub-stratosphere no longer offered immunity from fighter interception or anti-aircraft fire (flak), operating at an optimum 25,000ft would, it was hoped, considerably reduce the effectiveness of the latter. Both the B-17 and B-24 were limited in the load of bombs conveyed by the design of their bomb bays—roughly half that of the RAF 'heavies' at similar height and range. The advanced Norden bomb sight, a remarkable electro-mechanical computer, made possible very accurate strikes from high altitudes. The US Bomber Command was to employ both the B-17 and B-24, at that time coming in small numbers from the manufacturers but, as America's immense industrial capacity was turned to war production, soon in a greatly increased flow.

Eaker and Harris quickly established a good rapport, and although Eaker was frequently advised by well-meaning RAF seniors of the consequences of daylight bombing, he continued to pursue his brief from Arnold.

At the time Harris assumed command the average daily availability was 363 bombers, a situation not much different from that a year earlier. One encouraging sign was that heavy bomber production was improving and the re-equipping of Wellington and Hampden squadrons was taking place. Since the beginning of operations the normal crew of a Wellington or Whitley had been a first and second pilot, an observer and two wireless operator/air gunners, the observer acting as bomb-aimer. To maintain two pilots per bomber was putting a load on Operational Training Units, so that in March 1942 it was decided to dispense with the second pilot. A new position, that of flight engineer, was created by the coming of the four-engine 'heavies', and he was now to assist the pilot during take-off and landing. In fact, many flight engineers had the ability to pilot the aircraft in an emergency through cooperation with the pilot. A further rationalisation occurred in April 1942 when the observer was renamed the navigator and kept exclusively to that task, while a new post was created for bomb-aiming and manning the front turret (when necessary)—air bomber. The tasks of wireless operator and air gunner were also separated.

Below: No 408 Squadron, a Canadian-manned unit, was the last in Bomber Command to employ the Hampden on operations, the final sorties with the type being flown in September 1942. EQ:C is shown at its Balderton dispersal point in the hard winter of January 1942. Between June 1941 and September 1942 the squadron flew more than 1,200 sorties with Hampdens and lost 35. (IWM CH4737)

Above: Extraordinarily, the first Stirling and Halifax heavy bomber squadrons were expected to operate from turf-surfaced airfields. This was not a problem in summer, but these 30-ton giants rutted and churned up runways at other times of the year and were often bogged down. No 7 Squadron at Oakington was the first with Stirlings and suffered with unsuitable surface conditions for many months until concrete runways were laid. Until sufficient concrete hardstandings were available, the Stirlings at Oakington were lined up on the out-of-use runways for bombing up, as in this photograph taken in March 1942. W7466/ MG:B, with P Off M. R. Green and crew, failed to return from its sixth sortie, the Lübeck raid later in the month, crashing at Gnutz. The MG sports car is appropriate transport for a member of this squadron! (IWM CH5177)

Below: Two No 7 Squadron Stirlings cast shadows on Cambridgeshire fields on a blustery 10 April 1942. The leading aircraft is believed to be W7520/MG:S, which was lost in a collision with an Me 110 night fighter over Belgium the following month. MG:W is W7468, which survived until January 1944, when its undercarriage collapsed at Wratting Common. (IWM CH5495)

In the previous year a tour of operations was established as 30 raids. After at least a six-month rest period on non-operational duties, an airman was liable for recall to fly another twenty. Thereafter a permanent non-operational status was forthcoming unless a voluntary third tour was desired. While all aircrew must have been aware that the chances of getting killed were very high, the fact that one bomber failed to return for every 38 sorties flown in the past $2^1/_4$ years was known only to a few in the Command. Depending on the fortunes of an individual unit, morale had its ups and downs, yet overall it was good simply because the crews believed that what they were doing was vital to the war effort.

Harris lost little time in making his presence felt by doing the best he could with what forces he had. The first major raid was a precision attack on the Renault vehicle plant just outside Paris at Billancourt, mooted for some time and finally executed on 3/4 March 1942. In a maximum effort 235 aircraft were despatched, of which one Wellington failed to return. The target was well illuminated by flares and, since there was little in the way of ground fire to contend with, lower attack altitudes than normal were used.

Bombing was good, with an estimated 40 per cent destruction of the factory, halting production for over a month. Unfortunately, in the factory and surrounding area the bombs also took the lives of 367 French and badly injured an equal number. German propaganda exploited this aspect to the full. On the same night four Avro Lancasters carried out minelaying sorties, the début of an aircraft that would become famous.

With more than a hundred sets of Gee now available, the time had come to use this promising aid in a new technique code-named Shaker. Hitherto individual bomber crews were usually despatched at intervals, so that an operation extended over several hours. With Gee there was an opportunity to effect some concentration of effort, for the shorter the duration of the raid the less time for the enemy to exact a toll. The bombers were being sent in a planned stream. The system was first employed against Essen in the Ruhr on 8/9 March, when 211 aircraft, divided into three elements, were sent. The first group were to illuminate the target by dropping white flares at ten-second intervals along a six-mile stretch. The second wave of bombers carried incendiaries to mark the target for the third, main force, to bomb. The results were disappointing, with little sign of damage to this major industrial city. Eight bombers failed to return. Further raids employing Gee soon showed it to be a helpful aid to navigation, but it could do no more than provide guidance to the general target area.

The February directive had called for the greater use of incendiary bombs, which, as well as causing destruction by fire, if accurately placed also provided excellent target marking. The Germans appreciated this and became very adept at creating decoy fires which at times proved effective in drawing British bombs. The best defined targets at night were those on the coast, and Bomber Command planners decided that Lübeck, with its narrow streets and concentrated housing, would be highly susceptible to destruction by fire. By the light of a full moon, 234 aircraft set off on the night of 28 March for this Baltic port. They carried 144 tons of incendiaries, two-thirds of their total load, for this town known to have industries connected with U-boat equipment. Flak defences were light and many bombers attacked from as low as 2,000ft. The resulting conflagration is estimated to have destroyed half the buildings in the town proper, including a factory making oxygen apparatus for U-boats. Some 300 people were killed and around 800 injured.

The destruction of this historic medieval city so incensed the Nazi hierarchy that they ordered a series of bombings on historic locations in England (Bath, Canterbury, Exeter, Norwich and York) which came to be known as the Baedeker raids. In April similar fire damage was caused in four attacks on Rostock, another medieval city on the Baltic. Part of the force on each occasion was detailed to try and bomb the large Heinkel aircraft factory from low altitude, and though hits were obtained the disruption had only a minor effect on production. Raids on the Ruhr continued to bring very variable results for, despite the aid of Gee, bombs were sometimes delivered far from the assigned targets. Haze, natural and smoke-induced, made it very difficult to distinguish individual towns even on clear moonlit nights.

A high proportion of Bomber Command attacks were still directed at naval installations or support and production facilities, a continuing requirement in Air Ministry directives. The MAN works at Augsburg, identified as a major producer of submarine diesel engines, was seen as a target the destruction of which would greatly aid the battle against the U-boat. This required a precision attack, and success would most likely be obtained if the bombing was done in daylight. Harris decided to send No 5 Group's new Lancasters at low level to effect the necessary destruction. On 17 April 1942 twelve were despatched to fly below radar detection level while diversions by No 2 Group's Bostons with fighter escort would distract the Luftwaffe. Alas, the enemy was not tricked, and fighters intercepted the leading wave of Lancasters soon after crossing the French coast, shooting down four. Thereafter, once the bombers were through the coastal defence belt, no more fighters were encountered and the remaining eight aircraft reached the target. The flak defences had apparently been alerted, for heavy fire brought down three more of the bombers before they could escape into the gathering darkness. Though the plant was damaged, it later transpired that this was not the major source of U-boat engines that it had been thought.

Left, upper: A low-level reconnaissance picture of the damage to the Renault vehicle plant at Billancourt, west of Paris, following the night raid on 3/4 March 1942. The destruction wrought was later estimated to have denied the Germans some 2,300 vehicles. Tanks can be seen among the wreckage. (IWM C2279)

Left, lower: British airfields were cold places, particularly in winter and spring. Ground crew personnel often had little shelter at aircraft dispersal points, and at some stations they were allowed to erect shelters from any surplus material they could obtain. This 'erks'' shanty is at Gp Cpt Evan-Evans' Wellington station, March 1942. (IWM CH5130)

Far right: The old city of Lübeck under attack on the night of 28/29 March 1942. The large fires were thought to be in an enamelware factory. Lübeck was never again to be subjected to major assault by the RAF as, through a Swiss intermediary, it was agreed this port would be used for the shipment of Red Cross foods and material to Allied POWs. (IWM C2364)

Mindful that there were still rumblings about the resources allocated to Bomber Command and its ability to put them to good use in the cause of victory, Harris devised a plan for a raid involving a thousand bombers. Not only could this prove what was attainable with the optimum strength he sought, it could also bring a much needed lift to British morale at a time when the nation's fortunes seemed at low ebb. Both Portal and Churchill were taken with the idea. So was born the plan for Millenium, a thousand-sorties operation with an attack to be delivered in ninety minutes. The speed, height and timing of each aircraft was worked out to aid the concentration of bombing, to minimise collisions and to swamp the enemy defences. With an average maximum available strength of under 400 bombers, Harris looked to his Operational Training Units (OTUs) and to Coastal Command to provide a substantial part of the force. Aircraft and squadrons had been diverted to help Coastal Command and Harris felt some reciprocation should be forthcoming for this special effort, but he was unsuccessful because of an Admiralty veto. If it were to be achieved the total would have to come from within the Command, utilising its squadron reserve aircraft, plus some 350 aircraft mustered by its OTUs in Nos 91 and 92 Groups.

The raid required the benefit of moonlight, and the full-moon period fell at the end of May. For a week Harris husbanded his bombers with only light activity and that which should bring little loss, so that when weather conditions were right a thousand bombers could be launched against Hamburg. However, cloud protected the city, and while waiting for improvement in the weather he sent a small force of bombers against an aero-engine factory near Paris , which may also have been intended to allay any enemy suspicions that something unusual was afoot. Cloud was still forecast for the Hamburg area on the night of 30/31 May, so Cologne, where clear skies were predicted, was substituted as the target. By a supreme maintenance effort Bomber Command put up 677 bombers from its regular squadrons and 366 from its OTUs, and Flying Training Command contributed four, to make a total of 1,047. Those reaching the Cologne area dropped 1,455 tons of bombs, of which some two-thirds were incendiaries. An estimated 600 acres of the city were devastated and, of the several thousand casualties, more than 450 persons were killed. Bomber Command's loss was 41 aircraft ,of which 21 were Wellingtons, this type having made up well over half the force despatched. Despite fears of many collisions over the target, only one is known to have occurred.

Harris hoped to carry out a similar plundering of Essen, and his second 'Thousand Plan' raid was launched on 1/2 June 1942. Again using the OTUs, only 956 bombers could be despatched and once more haze and cloud came to Essen's rescue, causing the bombing to be widely scattered. A third 'Thou-sand Plan' raid was aimed at Bremen on 25/26 June. This time, through the target's naval connection, Coastal Command was permitted to participate, sending twenty Wellingtons and 82 Hudsons. The bottom of the barrel was being scraped to obtain the total of 1,067 aircraft as Blenheims, Bostons and even five Whitleys from Army Co-operation Command were enlisted. Considerable damage was done to industry and the attack was considered a success by Bomber Command, despite losses amounting to 53 aircraft, five of which were from Coastal Command. A particularly worrying aspect was the 23 aircraft lost by OTUs, an attrition in instructors and advanced course pilots which could not continue. For that reason, OTUs were henceforth rarely called upon to boost the regular bomber force.

That raid was also the last in which the troubled Manchester was involved, all squadrons operating this aircraft now being re-equipped with Lancasters. In September the No 5 Group Hampdens were withdrawn from regular operations and this organisation became an all-Lancaster force. Until April 1942 minelaying sorties had been exclusively No 5 Group's duties; this growing requirement was then being allocated to all operational groups. Heavy bomber production was at last accelerating, and from an average available strength of 42 at the beginning of 1942 it had risen to 261 by the end of the year. Moreover, while the overall aircraft strength was little better, bomb-carrying capacity had doubled.

East Anglia-based No 2 Group was shedding the last of its Blenheims and, apart from two Mosquito squadrons, the rest were getting American types—the nimble Boston and, later in the year, the larger Ventura and Mitchell mediums. The Ameri-

Left, upper: The first No 2 Group squadron to re-equip with Boston III light bombers was No 88 at Attlebridge. Faster, more manoeuvrable and with a tricycle undercarriage, the Boston proved very popular with pilots, if not navigators, who were sealed in their nose compartments. Sqn Ldr R. G. England had an appropriate slogan on his Z2229/RH:B, which had twenty raids to its credit at the time. On a number of occasions one Sgt R. England, a wireless operator, was also a member of the crew! (IWM CH7836)

Left, lower: Victim of a night fighter, No 214 Squadron's Stirling W7537/BU:H fell at Süstedt at 0204hrs on 4 June 1942 during a raid on Bremen. It is a fact that the wreckage from shot-down Allied bombers was taken as salvage to smelting works, later to be used in German aircraft production, the irony being that the RAF and USAAF helped supply the material that would be used against them. (IWM HU25742)

Below: With accompanying Mustang Is, AL749/RH:R and other No 88 Squadron Bostons fly close to the North Sea waves, a necessity if enemy radar was to be avoided. The Boston's bomb load was double that of the Blenheim and the aircraft was some 40mph faster. (IWM CH7844)

Right, upper: : Maintenance work on N3725/HA:D, of No 218 Squadron, at Downham Market in June 1942. In common with many other aircraft of the Gold Coast Squadron, it carried the name of a town in that country, in this case Mamprusi. At this time No 3 Group had six Stirling-equipped squadrons and there would be no expansion of the force until the following spring. The Stirling suffered the highest loss rate of the three four-engine bomber types, principally because of its poor ceiling, which made it more vulnerable to enemy defences. A cumbersome brute on the ground, it was, however, surprisingly manoeuvrable in flight. With one engine out of action it required careful handling; if two failed it did not want to remain in the sky. On its 31st operational sortie, on 14/15 September 1942, with P Off J. C. Frankcombe and crew, N3725 lost the starboard outer over Wilhemshaven. It was nursed back to the vicinity of home base, only to have the remaining engine on the starboard wing cease to function. The aircraft immediately did a wing-over and crashed near Stoke Ferry. Only the wirless operator and the mid-upper gunner survived, badly injured. (IWM CH17887)

Right, lower: The Vickers Wellington was the backbone of Bomber Command for three years. No 115 Squadron was one No 3 Group unit that did not convert to Stirlings, retaining its faithful Wellingtons until March 1943, when it was the first squadron in No 3 Group to convert to Lancasters. However, in flying more Wellington sorties than any other squadron in Bomber Command, it also suffered the highest losses with the type—more than a hundred, including crash-landings. X3662/KO:P was a survivor and after 36 raids was retired to serve with No 20 OTU. It was lost in a ditching off Skye on 8 October 1943. (IWM CH16994)

cans made their official début in borrowed Bostons on 4 July in a combined RAF/USAAF low-level raid on airfields in the Low Countries. Something of an Independence Day flag-waving gesture, it cost three of the twelve Bostons sent, two with US crews.

The first USAAF B-17Es were arriving in the United Kingdom at this time and the first mission of Eaker's VIII Bomber Command was despatched on 17 August to attack a rail yard at Rouen. With a sizeable escort of Spitfires, all twelve Fortresses returned safely. A further eight B-17 missions, all shallow penetrations, were without loss. Not until their tenth raid, on 6 September, did two bombers fail to return through com-

bat with fighters, by which date two more B-17 groups had become operational. However, one of these groups was stood down to form the basis of what the Americans termed a Combat Crew Replacement Center, basically an operational training unit, essential for the instruction of newly arrived crews in the flying control and other procedures in use in the UK.

A USAAF bomber group was a smaller organisation than that of an RAF bomber group, consisting of four squadrons, each, at the time, with a complement of nine aircraft. The authorised complement of an RAF bomber squadron with its reserves was exactly twice this, but the number of squadrons in an RAF bomber group could vary considerably, although

around a dozen was the usual strength. As VIII Bomber Command operations were organised on a group basis, the number of groups became the yardstick for strength assessment in the USAAF. At that time there were four squadrons with some 36 to 40 aircraft on an American bomber airfield, whereas those of the RAF supported two squadrons with aircraft establishments amounting to a similar total.

The USAAF wing organisation was the equivalent of the RAF group. The Eighth Air Force planned to field five full wings of fifteen groups each, four wings being equipped with B-17 Fortress and B-24 Liberator heavy bombers and the other with a mixed force of B-25 Mitchell and B-26 Marauder medium bombers. As the mediums had 48 aircraft per group, the total, if achieved, would be a staggering 3,420 bombers. Already a vast airfield building programme—one of the largest civil engineering projects undertaken in the UK—was under way in East Anglia , where the majority of the units would be based. The American air build-up was rapid during the autumn of 1942, for the Allies had now decided to invaded North-

West Africa with the object of eliminating enemy forces on that continent. The Eighth Air Force would have to furnish the US air element for this campaign by forming a new air force, the Twelfth, in the UK and taking the two most experienced B-17 groups. Meanwhile the heavy bombers could continue operations against targets in occupied Europe.

On 9 October VIII Bomber Command was, for the first time, able to despatch 108 bombers, two more bomb groups making their maiden missions this day, one equipped with the B-24 Liberator. The primary target was a steel works at Lille, the raid being strongly contested by the Luftwaffe. Four US bombers were lost and the air battles resulted in claims of more than a hundred enemy fighters destroyed by the air gunners. This being more than the entire strength of the Luftwaffe fighter units in the area, further interrogation of the gunners saw these claims reduced to 25 with 38 probable and 44 damaged, which was still an inflated total. In fact, but not known at the time, only two enemy fighters could be attributed to this air battle. Despite British ridicule about 'big-mouthed Yanks', this was

Top: Lancasters of No 83 Squadron taxi at Scampton for the 'Thousand Plan' raid on Bremen, 25/26 June 1942. In the foreground is R5620/OL:H, with P Off J. R. Farrow and crew, one member giving the V-sign. This aircraft had flown on the Squadron's first raid with Lancasters the previous month and was to be the only No 83 plane failing to return this night. Next is R5610/OL:G, another of the original Lancaster complement, which was lost soon after the squadron moved to Wyton to join the Pathfinders in August 1942. The third aircraft is R5565/OL:K, which survived until 21/22 January 1944, when it failed to return from Magdeburg. (IWM CH6095)

Left: A striking photograph taken during the 'Thousand Plan' raid on Bremen. Flares can be seen burning. The large flash is that of a flare dropped for photographic purposes and the circular effect is halation from perspex glass. (IWM C3064)
Right: The introduction of the Mk XIV bomb sight in 1942 gave improved accuracy in bombing, and the US-made version, the Model T1, became the standard instrument in Bomber Command to the end of the war. Introduction was slow as a different computer box was required for different aircraft types and a number of technical problems arose. (IWM CH14955)

Right: 'Uncle Sam''s 'heavies' join the fray. Watchers on the control tower at Grafton Underwood catch their first glimpse of the B-17s returning from the 17 August 1942 raid on Rouen marshalling yards. With hands in pockets, on the right, is Maj-Gen Carl Spaatz, commander of the Eighth Air Force and destined to head all USAAF strategic organisations engaged with Germany and its allies. The officer at the corner with a foot on the rail is believed to be Col Frank Castle, who would lose his life leading the largest Eighth Air Force mission of the war and posthumously be awarded the Medal of Honor. (USAAF)

not a case of deliberate false claims, but rather the problem of a score or more gunners shooting at the same fighter and each convinced his fire was responsible for its destruction.

The RAF still sent its heavy bombers out on the occasional daylight raid, bombing in the evening and returning under cover of darkness. In most cases these attempts at precision bomb-

ing were motivated by an upsurge in U-boat activity and appeals from the Admiralty and War Office for help. On 11 July 44 Lancasters undertook a 1,500-mile round trip to Danzig, taking a circuitous route across Denmark. Of those that found the target, two fell victim to flak, but fighters were not encountered. That effort was without success as little damage was done.

An equally unsatisfactory result came from the audacious raid on the Schneider heavy industry plant at Le Creusot on 17 October. Ninety-four No 5 Group Lancasters skirted the Brittany peninsula and hedge-hopped for 300 miles across France to find Le Creusot where, despite climbing to between 2,000 and 7,000ft for accurate sighting, the bombs mostly fell short. A number of French civilian casualties resulted. Returning in darkness helped keep losses to a single Lancaster, and that aircraft was believed to have collided with a building when flying low.

The light and medium bombers proved more successful in a daylight raid on the Philips radio factory at Eindhoven in Holland. Intelligence had information that radio and radar components were being supplied to the Germans from there. No 2 Group put up a maximum effort with 47 Venturas, 36 Bostons and 10 Mosquitos on 6 December, a Sunday being selected in the hope of limiting casualties among Dutch factory workers. Three waves of bombers went in at low level to avoid radar detection, for the target was beyond fighter escort range. A B-17 raid over northern France did not divert all the Luftwaffe's attention, for its fighters were responsible for most of the fourteen bombers that failed to return. Much of the bombing was very accurate and the destruction wrought halted production for several months. Unfortunately, the measures taken to minimise civilian casualties were not very effective and most of the 150 persons killed were Dutch.

Left, upper: B-17E 12578, of the 340th Bomb Squadron, in its landing roll at Grafton Underwood after returning from Rouen. The pilot was Maj Paul Tibbets, who three years later would fly the B-29 delivering the first atom bomb on Japan. Also on board was Col Frank Armstrong, CO of the 97th Bomb Group. (USAAF)

Left, lower: The first USAAF bomber group equipped with B-24D Liberators arrived in the United Kingdom in September 1942 and a second—less one squadron—in October. With a better range and load capability, the type was in great demand, particularly for anti-submarine work. Consequently pressing requirements elsewhere resulted in no more B-24 units becoming operational in the UK for eleven months, and those already on hand were often diverted to other tasks or detached to North Africa. *Teggie Ann*, 123754, seen here under service at Alconbury, was usually flown by the 93rd Bomb Group CO or his deputy. The bomber's career was terminated when the aircraft was crash-landed in Turkey in August 1943. (USAAF)

In addition to these occasional special large-scale daylight attacks by Bomber Command 'heavies' and No 2 Group, the latter made many small-scale raids, mostly at port installations and airfields in the occupied countries within range. Throughout 1942 regular harassing daylight raids into Germany were made by one or two aircraft using heavy overcasts as cover. Scuttle was the code name for those sorties where the aircraft was given free range over a selected area. Moling was the use of Gee to bomb a specific target using complete or near cloud cover. Similar activities were conducted at night, with the purpose of alerting the enemy defences and bringing general concern to civilians.

The night remained Bomber Command's main period of activity, but the cloak of darkness that once offered the best security was pierced by the defences with widening success. Airborne radar was now being carried by the enemy night fighters, enabling them to close with the bombers, where their cannon armament outranged the .303s of their quarries. Average bomber losses crept higher, to run at 4 per cent of sorties by the end of the year. Seeking to reduce the trend, Bomber Command looked to countermeasures, notably radio and radar, that were under development. The first, named Shiver, was the jamming of the enemy's Würzburg radars. Then came Mandril, the

ground stations in the UK that transmitted to jam Freya radar. Introduced in December 1942, it did not appear to have any significant effect. An airborne version was introduced at a later date. In the same month, selected bombers began using Tinsel, broadcasting engine noise on the same wavelength as intercepted ground-to-air radio traffic.

While some notable improvements in the effectiveness of Bomber Command's attacks had come about during the first months of Harris's leadership, bombs were still too often going astray, particularly under cloudy conditions. Crews specialised in leading night raids had been advocated for some time, and this evolved into the idea of a Target Finding Force, generally attributed to its most ardent promoter, Group Captain S. O. Bufton. Deputy Director Bomber Operations on the Air Ministry staff in 1942, he had practical experience in bombers as an early wartime CO of No 4 Group. He proposed that the Target Finding Force should be composed of six squadrons stationed in the same area and that a third of the crews should be the most experienced in the Command.

Harris was not in favour of what he saw as an élite establishment, but Portal approved and eventually agreement was reached to take one squadron from each group, basing them in the western area of No 3 Group and under its auspices. Air

Above: The first Royal Canadian Air Force squadron formed in Bomber Command was No 405, flying Wellingtons operationally from June 1941 until April 1942, when it converted to Halifaxes. Here, back from a flight, the weary crew of W7802/LQ:Q enter RAF transport at Topcliffe in September 1942. While the rear gunner extracts himself from his turret his parachute is held by a ground crewman. Placing a parachute on the ground was taboo, even in dry conditions, as destructive pests might enter it. The chest pack was standard for RAF bomber crews and, while easily snapped on to the harness, might not be quickly located in darkness or in an emergency. This Halifax and its regular crew, captained by Sgt J. T. Campbell, failed to return from the Flensburg raid of 1/2 October 1942. (IWM CH6642)

Below: The spacious bomb bay of a No 207 Squadron Lancaster, prepared for the mission to Düsseldorf on 12/13 September 1942. Code words were used in loading directions from Command, and this is a 4,000lb HC 'Cookie' with twelve containers of incendiaries coded 'Usual'. With the 4,000lb HC and maximum number of 500lb bombs the code-word was 'Normal' and for the 4,000lb HC and 1,000lb bombs 'Abnormal'. There was a whole series of different bomb mixes, including the maximum incendiary load known as 'Arson'. (IWM CH17458)

Commodore Donald Bennett, who before the war had distinguished himself through a number of long-range flights, was put in command of what Harris decided to call the Pathfinder Force (PFF). With a brief to find and mark targets for the main force bombers, the Pathfinders took up station on 17 August and with no special training were sent on their first operation in the late evening of the following day.

Above: The first Royal Canadian Air Force heavy bomber squadron received Halifaxes in April 1942. During the first few months operational attrition was severe and few Halifaxes flew more than a dozen sorties before loss or transfer. This photograph shows armourers attaching incendiary clusters to the wing racks of Halifax Mk II W7802/LQ:Q on a bleak autumn afternoon at Topcliffe. A limitation of the Halifax was its shallow bay. Although an 8,000lb HC bomb was dropped on one occasion and a total of four hundred and sixty-seven 4,000lb HC bombs on other raids, no bombs larger than 2,000lb were carried operationally after 1942. (IWM: CH6625)

Left: Lancasters over the French countryside of evening shadows while en route to the Schneider heavy engineering factory at Le Creusot, 17 October 1942. The nearest aircraft in the photograph is R5497/OF:Z of No 97 Squadron, with Fg Off J. R. Brunt and crew. Their luck ran out on the night of 17/18 December 1942 when, in the same Lancaster, they were one of nine crews who failed to return that night. (IWM C3183)

Above: Back from another trip, torches lodged in flying boots, men of a No 57 Squadron crew converse with ground personnel at Scampton. Shoulder flashes show two of the airmen to be Canadian and another a New Zealander, illustrating the mix of nationalities commonplace with Bomber Command crews. W4201/ DX:F was the No 57 CO's personal aircraft, in which he led the Squadron's first Lancaster operation on 12/13 October 1942 to Wismar. It was eventually written off in a crash-landing at home station after being badly shot up by a night fighter on 13/14 March 1943. (IWM CH8803)

For many nights, until better aids became available, PFF activity rarely showed advantages. The pattern that evolved was for the first contingent to illuminate the target area with numerous white flares. The next identified aiming points and released coloured parachute flares, red, green or yellow. The third wave of Pathfinders would bomb on these target indicators with incendiaries. For the Nuremberg attack on 28/29 August the Pathfinders used a new target indicator, a 250lb bomb case filled with a benzol-rubber-phosphorus mix. At Düsseldorf on 10/11 September, 2,800lb of similar material in a 4,000lb bomb case was used, its distinctive display earning it the name Pink Pansy. A further development, first used on 16 January 1943, was a 250lb target indicator that released a cascade of the required colours just before striking the ground, thus giving a more precise aiming point.

But the biggest step in furthering the accurate marking of target by the PFF was the introduction of Oboe. This radar pulse system used two mother stations transmitting to an aircraft. Apparatus in the aircraft returned a signal, allowing the ground stations to give a precise indication of position. Its main drawbacks were that, being a line-of-sight device, its range was limited to 300 miles and that the number of Oboe-equipped aircraft that could be controlled was limited to sixteen per hour.

Under the code name Trinity, Oboe had its early trials in Stirlings against Brest to avoid penetration over ground where a loss might put the equipment into enemy hands before it was ready for full-scale use. Then Oboe was installed in Mosquitos, which, having a 30,000ft ceiling, could achieve maximum range extension. PFF Mosquitos began a series of trials on 20/21 December 1942, and while the accuracy of this device was evident, many equipment failures marred its introduction. Even so, despite a shaky beginning, the potential of the PFF was plain to see.

On 8 January 1943 the PFF was given group status, Bennett becoming AOC-in-C of a new No 8 Group. At the beginning of the same month the nine Canadian squadrons which No 4 Group had fostered were gathered into the specially created No 6 Group, with north Yorkshire airfields as its domain.

Left, upper: : Flare lanes over Genoa, 22/23 October 1942, when 112 No 5 Group Lancasters opened a campaign against Italian industrial cities for both physical and moral support for the Axis forces in North Africa, against whom the Allies had started action to defeat. There were no losses and the raid was rated as highly successful. (IWM C3192)

Left, lower: One of the most successful raids by No 2 Group's light and medium bombers was that on the Philips works at Eindhoven on 6 December 1942. It required a 65-mile penetration of enemy-occupied territory and was beyond Spitfire escort range. Why Army Co-operation Command Mustangs were not used on this and other similar occasions is an unresolved mystery. (IWM C3268)

Above right: Apart from the 97th, all Fortress groups arriving in Britain during the late summer and autumn of 1943 were equipped with the improved B-17F model. As in RAF Bomber Command, it was policy to assign a crew to a specific aircraft in which, unless it were unserviceable or under repair, they would normally fly their missions. Seen here taxying on the perimeter track at Molesworth on 25 January 1943, 124559/PU:C, *Ooold Soljer*, of the 360th Bomb Squadron, 303rd Bomb Group, was the personal aircraft of Capt Lewis Lyle and crew. While flown by another crew it was involved in a collision with another B-17 while assembling a formation on 31 March 1943, crashing near Wellingborough. Lewis Lyle went on to complete two tours, his 70 combat missions being surpassed by only one other Eighth Air Force bomber pilot. (USAAF)

In late October 1942 RAF Bomber Command had been directed to a series of attacks on industrial cities in northern Italy, a move in support of the North African offensives. These raids continued periodically for some weeks, and in January, after a fourteen-month absence, Berlin was attacked on consecutive nights. On both occasions the PFF failed and bombing was scattered, evidence that, beyond Gee guidance, raids against distant targets were still circumspect. Much effort was expended against targets connected with the U-boat war, and in January Bomber Command was directed to conduct full-scale area attacks on the four French coast bases of Lorient, St Nazaire, Brest and La Pallice. Here the U-boats were protected by immense concrete shelters, impervious to anything Bomber Command could drop on them at this stage of hostilities, and the attacks were soon recognised at fruitless and only damaging to French people and property.

VIII Bomber Command had also been given these ports as immediate priority targets, which was even more misguided in view of the fact that the most powerful bomb that could be carried by the Fortresses was 2,000lb and incapable of penetrating the protective concrete structures. The two most experienced B-17 groups had been withdrawn for participation in the North African invasion early in November 1942, leaving four B-17 groups, three of which had only become operational that month. Two B-24 groups were also on hand, but one had only three squadrons and part of the other was diverted to help Coastal Command before being temporarily detached to operate in North Africa.

Operating B-17 and B-24 formations together had proved difficult due to dissimilar aircraft performance. The remaining B-24s were therefore confined to diversions or following the B-17 force, which proved the most vulnerable location for fighter interceptions. Throughout the winter months it was the B-17s that pioneered VIII Bomber Command's daylight bombing tactics. High-altitude precision bombing was all very well in the predictable blue skies of continental United States, but north-western European weather rarely gave clear skies and often only fleetingly in winter. Weather was the major obstacle to high-altitude precision bombing. After the low losses of early missions the B-17 formations began to encounter increasing opposition. An attack on St Nazaire by 60 B-17s on 3 January 1943 saw seven lost for claims of fourteen of the enemy. Whatever the validity of the gunners' claims, it was clear that the force could not endure losses of 10 per cent for long, albeit that the average loss for the first four months was 2.54 per cent.

While Harris, Portal and other senior British air leaders still believed that the Americans would have to turn to night bombing, they had come to support their new ally in the venture. They were in no mind to give the sceptics of the bombing offensive grounds for furthering their misgivings. However, the doubts of some of Churchill's advisers had caused the Prime Minister to ask President Roosevelt to have the USAAF bombers in Britain turned to night operations. With such influential opposition, the US Army staff present at the Casablanca conference sent for General Eaker, who had no prior warning of exactly why he was summoned. Once the situation had been explained by General Arnold, Eaker produced a short written brief for Churchill, handed to him at a private meeting between the two. Impressed, Churchill withdrew his request to the President and, while not entirely convinced that daylight bombing would be successful, he was prepared to give his support for the time being. It is said that Eaker's statement, that sending the RAF by night and the Eighth Air Force by day would result in round-the-clock bombing, delighted the Prime Minister.

At the Casablanca conference the Combined Chiefs of Staff issued the first directive combining the objectives for both RAF Bomber Command and the Eighth Air Force. The first priority was U-boat construction and port facilities, the second the enemy air force, the third transportation and the fourth oil. The bombing campaign was defined as a prelude to the Allied invasion of Europe to reduce German industrial and military might, but there were still those who hoped that strategic bombing alone might have a more direct effect in the quest for victory.

5
THE OFFENSIVE
GATHERS WEIGHT

Eaker, to endorse his pledge of round-the-clock bombing, despatched his Fortresses and Liberators to a German target for the first time on 27 January 1943. The target was to have been the submarine construction yards at Vegesack near Bremen but, due to unfavourable weather forecasts, Wilhelmshaven naval base was substituted as the primary objective. A maximum effort put 64 B-17s and 27 B-24s into the winter sky, only to have cloud deflect several of the raiders. Even so, 55 B-17s unloaded 255 'thousand-pounders' on the port with the loss of only one B-17 of the attacking force despite the appearance of several Me 109s. Fighter opposition was more determined a week later, when 65 B-17s went to Emden and lost five of their number. On St Valentines' Day the Eighth Air Force attempted its first in-strength

thrust into the Ruhr, with Hamm marshalling yard as the target, only to have cloud force an abandonment. The US bombers had to wait until 4 March before another strike at Hamm could be mounted. Sixteen of the 71 B-17s sent were able to bomb, 46 of the rest diverting to Rotterdam docks when once again cloud frustrated the original scheme. Four B-17s of the group that attacked were lost and nine damaged, underlining tha fact that the Ruhr was no place for such a small lone formation.

During the first three months of 1943 the Eighth Air Force received few replacement crews or aircraft and suffered a 7.5 per cent average loss rate to sorties flown in January and 8.1 per cent in February—a rate which, if sustained, would soon eliminate the entire force. The average effective strength of VIII Bomber Command had declined from 115 'heavies' in December 1942 to 84 two months later. Replacement was not the only problem for Eaker in the early months of 1943: his only fighter group capable of 300 miles' radius of action support for the bombers had all its P-38 Lightnings transferred to North Africa to make up losses in Twelfth Air Force units. Two new B-17 groups in the USA, scheduled to join the Eighth Air Force in January and February, were diverted to North Africa and there was a demand from that war zone for two of the B-17 groups in England to be sent there. This latter was successfully resisted. A few replacements improved matters in March and April but, until May 1943, the four B-17 groups constituted the main active combat force.

In the course of the winter operations these units developed the standing operating procedures for Eighth Air Force heavy bomber operations, which remained little changed to the end of the war. To improve strike concentrations, the bomb-aiming was moved from the leading aircraft of a three-plane flight to a six-plane squadron formation, and then to the bombardier of the group lead-plane, all 18, 21 or 27 aircraft that composed the group formation dropping on his release. This naturally led to the most accomplished bombardiers, navigators and pilots manning lead aircraft. A standard formation that

Below: In enemy colours. B-17F 124585/PU:B, *Wulf Hound*, was shot up by fighters on the 12 December 1942 mission and Lt Paul Flickinger landed the damaged aircraft at Leeuwarden. Six of the crew evaded capture but in addition to four prisoners the Luftwaffe was presented with an easily repaired

Fortress. This was the first of about a dozen B-17s and B-24s the Luftwaffe would acquire and make airworthy, using them for clandestine operations. Most types of British bomber were also captured and flown, including the Blenheim, Wellington, Stirling and Lancaster. (S. Clay 2)

Above: Of some sixty Lancasters and Mosquitos involved in an experimental Oboe pathfinder attack over cloud-shrouded Essen on 13/14 January 1943, four bombers failed to return. Two of these were from No 106 Squadron, whose aircraft appear to have been intercepted by freelancing *Wilde Sau* FW 190s. Another of the squadron's Lancasters had a lucky escape thanks to the evasive action taken by pilot Sgt P. N. Reed. Soon after leaving the target the bomber was suddenly raked from tail to nose by cannon and machine-gun fire from an FW 190. The fighter made a second attack, scoring several strikes on the Lancaster. Rear gunner Sgt G. A. V. Twinn was severely wounded and the mid-upper gunner Sgt J. B. Hood killed by the enemy fire. Reed brought his crippled aircraft, R5700/ZN:G, in for a crash-landing at the USAAF base at Hardwick. Repaired, the Lancaster was issued to No 9 Squadron, with whom it was lost in the Hanover raid of 22/23 September 1943. (IWM CE4)

rons in a group. At a predetermined landmark some 25 to 50 miles from the target, the formation would turn for the bomb run, the groups going into trail. Beyond the target another turn would be made to re-establish the defensive alignment of the group formations.

Luftwaffe fighter pilots found these tight formations, putting out volumes of .50in calibre fire, difficult and dangerous to engage. New tactics had to be worked out and one solution was to make frontal passes, where both B-17s and B-24s were less well defended and the opportunity to kill or disable the pilots was presented. Once this tactic was recognised the Americans hastily improvised additional gun positions in the noses of their bombers for hand-held weapons, while requesting power-operated turrets in later models of both the B-17 and B-24. The fact was that, thanks to the rate of closure, accurate sighting for the fighters making a frontal attack was difficult to achieve, particularly if the target bomber took evasive action. For this reason most Luftwaffe fighter units dispensed with this form of attack in preference to the more effective rear approach.

On 18 March VIII Bomber Command was, for the first time, able to demonstrate what could be achieved by its form of bombing. In a clear sky, 97 of 103 B-17s and B-24s despatched

would combine manoeuvrability with good defence evolved from various trials. Three-plane flights of a nine-plane squadron were flown one high, one low on the lead and staggered back. The three squadrons of a group were echeloned in similar fashion so that the whole group formation took the form of an angled wedge. This permitted the maximum number of defence positions a clear field of fire and also allowed the high and low squadrons to slide from one side to the other when making turns, thus retaining the compactness of the group formation. Further to enhance defence, three groups were often flown as a combat wing, positioned relative to the squad-

dropped 268 short tons of high explosive on the Vegesack U-boat yards. Reconnaissance brought photographic evidence that 76 per cent of the bombs struck within 1,000ft of the aiming point. Seven U-boats received severe damage and many buildings were destroyed. However, such precise bombing was more the exception than the rule during these early missions, and occasionally it was disastrously astray. The Ford plant at Antwerp was intended for 245 tons aimed by 82 B-17s and B-24s on 5 April. The lead group came under fighter attack on the bomb run and the leader was hit, causing an inaccurate bomb release from which others took their cue to drop. The bombs struck a residential district, killing 936 and injuring 1,342 civilians. Precision bombing over Germany, too, would frequently cause civilian casualties by default.

While the Eighth Air Force struggled on without expansion, RAF Bomber Command was getting into its stride. In contrast to the Eighth's 526 sorties and 636 short tons dropped during February, Bomber Command put up 4,939 sorties and dispensed 12,274 short tons of ordnance. This was in part due to its no longer being restricted to operating in the full-moon period, thanks to the Pathfinders and their radar aids.

By March 1943 Bomber Command had more than 600 aircraft on strength, over 400 being heavy four-engine types. Using the remarkable accuracy of Oboe, Harris believed he had the means to do real harm to the Ruhr industrial cities and commenced a campaign he would later term the Battle of the Ruhr. At this time he was aware that if strategic bombing was to have a positive effect, or bring about a collapse of the German war effort, he had only about a year to achieve his aim before control of the bomber forces was turned over to the Supreme Allied Commander ready for the planned cross-Channel invasion.

In order that the enemy did not reinforce his defences of the Ruhr by transferring fighters and flak units from other areas, the bombing attacks were interspersed with those on such far-spread targets as Kiel, Berlin, Pilsen and St Nazaire. Using the Oboe pathfinder Mosquitos, target-marking could be made with the likelihood of only a 300yd margin of error. But Oboe's initial problem was equipment failure. Accurate Oboe-assisted marking over Essen on 5/6 March brought the city its most devastating raid so far, with extensive damage to the giant Krupps armaments works.

The pathfinder technique was one of continuing development and variation. Mosquitos released parachute-held sky markers when cloud obscured a target and ground markers when conditions were clear. Routes were also marked with coloured flares. The heavy pathfinder aircraft were generally employed in renewing the original marking locations every few minutes. The Germans often endeavoured to deploy decoy markers, which required frequent changes in pathfinder procedures and the kind of target indicators used. In fact, by the end of hostilities, more than 40 different target indicators and associated pyrotechnics had been developed.

In 22 major raids during March and April and up to mid-May 1943, RAF Bomber Command despatched an average of 440 bombers in its mounting campaign. Yet in the same period the defences were also advancing their arts, taking an increasing toll of the bombers. During these same 22 raids the average loss per night was eighteen aircraft, equivalent to the complete complement of one bomber squadron! A new individual high occurred on 16/17 April, when nearly 600 bombers were divided between targets at Pilsen and Mannheim, 54 failing to return from the night's operations, including several ditching in the sea short of fuel.

Right: During an attack by Venturas on Abbeville marshalling yards on 3 February 1943, a few FW 190s intercepted. This photograph captures one as it dives away after delivering its attack. (IWM C3324)

Right: A Ventura of No 21 Squadron, AE742/YH:M, with W Off L. L. G. Jones and crew, during an attack on the blast furnaces and steelworks at Ijmuiden on 13 February 1943. None of the 34 aircraft sent was lost. A month later AE742 suffered flak damage and was ditched near Guernsey. (IWM C3404)

Above: A helping hand from an ally: British mechanics work on the refurbishment of B-17F 41-24502/BO:V in a Burtonwood hangar. Burtonwood became a Base Air Depot with more than 11,000 British and US personnel working on a range of aircraft repair, servicing and modification. This Fortress was an original combat aircraft of the 368th Bomb Squadron at Thurleigh and served with that unit until being crash-landed at Sudborne, Suffolk, on return from the 28 July 1943 mission to Kassel. (IWM D11800)
Left: Sqn Ldr W. N. Dixon DFC takes a look at the outer starboard Merlin of No 76 Squadron Halifax W7813/MP:E, *Edward the Great,* which powered the bomber for 32 raids and some 200 hours—a feat considered something of a record when most Halifax Merlins had to be changed at half that total. Sqn Ldr Dixon flew this aircraft on 8/9 March 1943, its last sortie with No 76. Thereafter, following major overhaul, it was transferred to No 77 Squadron and lost on the 25/26 May 1943 Düsseldorf raid. (IWM CH9332)

The Luftwaffe was not only expanding its night fighter force; some day fighter units were transferred to the west in order to meet an upsurge in USAAF activity. In the second week of May 1943, Eaker's bomber availability had more than doubled. Four new B-17 groups had arrived from the USA in mid-April, another re-formed from an OTU in England, and a group of B-26 Marauders was also ready for action. Between May and August 1943 the Eighth Air Force would receive seven more B-17, one B-24 and three B-26 groups, raising its effective strength to more than 600, of which 200 were B-26 mediums. The complement of a medium bomber group was 64 aircraft, while that for the heavy bombers had now been increased to 40.

The Marauders were not long for VIII Bomber Command. They had been used quite successfully in low-level operations in the south-west Pacific war zone, with relatively low losses. However, the opposition there was not as practised or substantial as that encountered in western Europe. The type's début came on 14 May when a dozen attempted a low-level attack on the power station at Ijmuiden, Holland. Photographic reconnaissance showed no damage to the target and three days later the Marauders were sent to try again. Of the eleven B-26s despatched, one turned back with suspected mechanical trouble. The ten left to attack not only failed to find the target but also failed to return. Thereafter the only operational Marauder group was stood down while tactics were reviewed. Eaker would have preferred more B-17s and B-24s to the short-range B-26s. To underline the type's unsuitability for the strategic bombing offensive, the B-26 groups were transferred to VIII Air Support Command. When Marauders resumed operations in late July, they flew in tight formations at medium altitudes, 10,000 to 14,000ft, attacking airfields and enemy installations in the European coastal belt. Thus employed, they were reasonably successful and usually suffered little. In October VIII Air Support Command HQ became the new Ninth Air Force HQ and the Marauders were transferred to this tactical air force being formed for the planned invasion of the continent the following year. In a similar move, at the end of May 1943 RAF Bomber Command transferred No 2 Group with its Bostons and Mitchells to Fighter Command prior to the formation of a British air contingent for the invasion plan.

The Marauder débâcle of 17 May was veiled by the spectacular attack on the Ruhr dams the previous night. Through the novelty, skill and courage involved, this raid became the most famous Bomber Command operation of the war, yet it had little overall effect upon German's war economy if bringing considerable disruption of life and damage to property by flood in the immediate areas of the successful breaches. The means of destroying the dams was Upkeep, a special 'bouncing bomb'—more a large, spinning depth charge—designed by Barnes Wallis of Vickers-Armstrong, the manufacturers of the Wellington. Harris was initially hostile to the idea, yet, when eventually persuaded, formed a special squadron to train and carry out the task. Bright moonlight was required, with approaches a few feet above the dam waters. On the night of 16/17 May, nineteen Lancasters were despatched with the Mohne, Eder, Sorpe and Schwelme dams as targets. Five aircraft were lost en route, the Mohne and Eder were successfully breached and three more Lancasters were brought down after bombing. An estimated 130 million gallons of water were released, causing some 1,300 casualties and widespread damage and disruption of services. Although attacked, the Sorpe dam was known to be unlikely to give, because of its sturdy construction, but this held the reservoir which if released would have had greater effect upon the Ruhr industries.

Despite the loss of nearly half the force, Harris retained the dam-busting squadron for special low-level precision operations. His main concern at this time was the continuing upward trend in losses to the main force engaged in hammering the Ruhr. In 21 major raids between mid-May and mid-July, 422 bombers were lost but with more than ten thousand sorties during this period the loss rate stood at just over 4 per cent. Nevertheless, Command strength was continually expanding, with the formation of new squadrons and a start being made on raising their establishment from 16 to 24 aircraft. By mid-July the total of assigned squadrons was 66, and this advanced to 75 by the end of the year, even if not all were fully operational.

The Command's gathering strength enabled Harris to send 826 bombers to Dortmund on 23/24 May and 883 to Düsseldorf and Münster on 11/12 June, but these were the highest totals for some months. Night fighters were freelancing at the target and as opposition grew in the later stages of an attack it was evident that the enemy was drawing in his fighters from over a wide area. A counter-action to this was to have smaller numbers of bombers over a target in a shorter time. Plane-over-target times were increased from 10 to 30 per minute, despite the increased risk of collision and aircraft being struck by the bombs of higher aircraft.

A new tactic was employed on 20/21 June when 60 Lancasters raided Friedrichshafen and then flew on to land at airfields in North Africa. Although no losses were incurred, difficulties with maintenance and supply at distant bases tended to negate the advantages. More direct countermeasures had to be taken in an effort to reduce bomber losses, and the most significant was introduced in late July.

Hamburg, Germany's second largest city and major port, had been attacked many times during the past four years and been selected for sustained attack by the bomber forces in the early spring of 1943. In the final days of July the plan was put

Above: The head of a column of 21 Fortresses that the 91st Bomb Group launched from Bassingbourn on 22 March 1943 for a mission to Wilhelmshaven. First is 124459/LL:B, *Hellsapoppin*, second 25763/LL:F, *Bomb Boggie*, and third 124484/LL:C, *The Bad Egg*, all of the 401st Bomb Squadron. These three returned this day; one in the line-up did not. *Hellsapoppin* went down on the Bremen raid of 17 April, five of the crew being killed and five made prisoner; *Bomb Boggie* failed to return on 6 September but the crew survived; and *The Bad Egg* made a crash-landing at Andrews Field on the last day of the year, killing the driver of a jeep in the process. (USAAF)

Left: Capt John C. Bishop (second right), 323rd Bomb Squadron Operations Officer, with 1/Lt Charles H. Silvernail (left, with arm raised) and his crew, back from Wilhelmshaven, 22 March 1943. The manufacturer's frontal armament provision for the B-17F was a single rifle-calibre machine gun which could be moved to one of three sockets in the plexiglass nose. This was impractical and of little value. In-the-field modifications improved forward firepower, and this Fortress has a .50-calibre Browning in the upper right gun socket and another through a side window for use by the navigator. B-17F 25077/OR:T, *Delta Rebel 2nd,* completed its 21st operational sortie on this date, a higher total than any other Fortress in the Eighth Air Force up to this time. (USAAF)

into action. For the first time Window, the code name for an anti-radar device, was used. This consisted of large quantities of metallic-coated paper strips which were dropped by the raiders to swamp the gunlaying Würzburg radars with false echoes. Developed the previous year, its use had hitherto been banned for fear that the Germans would use it against the British radar defences. The series of attacks on Hamburg was opened on the night of 24/25 July when 791 aircraft were sent, with the loss of only twelve. On 27/28 July 787 went and seventeen were lost, and on 29/30 July of 777 despatched 28 went down. While a final raid on 2/3 August by 740 aircraft was frustrated by bad weather, it also brought the heaviest loss of 30.

The devastation caused was enormous, with great fires raging out of control. On the second night unusually warm weather had caused a firestorm, a condition where the air becomes so hot that its specific weight decreases, causing high winds by sucking in surrounding, cooler air, the enormous differences in temperatures causing the storm phenomena. An estimated 74 per cent of this city was utterly destroyed, with every service put out of action. Economically, Hamburg was destroyed. More chilling was the deaths of some 40,000 of its inhabitants, most from carbon monoxide poisoning caused by the fires. The firestorms were an unexpected result of the attack, but the destruction of Hamburg made the German authorities fear that if the bombers could bring the same level of destruction to other major cities, national morale might be severely strained. The July 1943 Hamburg missions were the nearest that advocates of bombing to break morale came to their goal, for RAF Bomber Command was never able to create such horrific destruction again before the cross-Channel invasion was launched.

In addition to the 2,355 RAF bombers thought to have attacked Hamburg, the Eighth Air Force put a total 154 B-17s over the smoking city on 25 and 26 July. This was the first direct cooperation between the Eighth Air Force and RAF Bomber Command to meet the Combined Bomber Offensive Directive known as Pointblank. The smoke interfered with the American bomb-aiming on both occasions, and thereafter they tried to avoid attacking a target which had been hit by the RAF the night before. The Eighth Air Force's contribution to the destruction of Hamburg came in a week of intensive activity for the Fortresses.

During May and June the American bombers had been continually frustrated by cloud in their attempts to carry out precision attacks. Of eighteen missions flown since VIII Bomber Command doubled its strength in May, only seven were to targets in Germany and only one of those into the Ruhr, where heavy damage was rendered to a tyre factory at Hüls. Bombing was often good at other targets but the restrictions imposed by weather caused Eaker and his commanders to look again at night operations, committing one Fortress squadron to training and actually participating in the RAF's night bombing raids. Interest was also focused on the British 'blind bombing' radars with the aim of procuring sufficient to install in B-17s and B-24s acting as pathfinders when extensive undercast clouds were encountered. Gee had already been acquired for lead aircraft and the intention was progressively to equip more of the 'heavies' with this excellent navigational aid. It was planned to form a special pathfinder group which would use Oboe and H2S until the US-built version of the latter, H2X, was available. Meanwhile the Eighth's bombers had to wait for fine weather, and in late July the prognosis was for a high-pressure period—which indeed came to pass. Taking full advantage of clear skies, Eaker sent his bombers out with only one break in the succession of missions that became known in the Eighth Air Force as Blitz Week.

The initial attacks on 24 July involved the Americans' first strikes at targets in Norway with 180 B-17s of the 1st Wing against Heroya and 129 of the 4th Wing against Trondheim

Above: Many a Wellington returned from operations minus parts of its fabric skin through enemy action. A direct hit from flak when approaching Duisburg on 8/9 April 1943 blasted away the rear turret with gunner and caused other severe damage to this No 428 Squadron aircraft. The pilot, Sgt L. F. Williamson, found that he could still control the aircraft, so he continued to the target. After bombing it was found that hydraulic power had been lost and that the bomb doors could not be closed. Despite this difficulty and the near-naked rear end, HE239/NA:Y was brought back for a safe landing at West Malling. The Wellington was repaired and pensioned off to fly with OTUs for the rest of its life. (IWM CH9867)

Below: A ground spectator's view of an Eighth Air Force bomb group strike: the detonation of over a hundred 1,000lb GPs on and around the Focke-Wulf factory at Bremen, 17 April 1943. Extensive damage was done to the factory but fighter production had been transferred to other sites some months beforehand in anticipation of bombing raids. (IWM HU25798)

and Bergen. The 4th Wing had begun operations in May and both wings soon grew in size to become redesignated as divisions. There was good bombing at Heroya, but cloud caused the Bergen force to bring their loads home. Losses amounted to ten. Next day, while part of the B-17 force went to Hamburg, others went to Kiel, with total losses nineteen out of 323 despatched. Hanover and Hamburg targets brought stiff opposition on the 26th, causing 24 Fortresses to be lost. Aircraft plants at Kassel and Oschersleben were the targets on 28 July, when fierce air battles resulted in 22 Fortresses failing to return. Next day, while the 1st Wing attacked Kiel shipyards, the 4th Wing made an accurate strike on the Heinkel works at Warnemünde for the loss of ten B-17s.

The final missions of Blitz Week were against aircraft works at Kassel. On that day, when twelve B-17s failed to return, P-47 Thunderbolt fighters probably helped to reduce losses by providing support as far as the German border, their increased range made possible by auxiliary fuel tanks. The Luftwaffe chose to leave its main assault on the US bomber formations until they were beyond the radius of action that escort fighters normally achieved. On this occasion the Thunderbolts' claims of 25 enemy fighters destroyed suggests that the Luftwaffe did not expect to see the P-47s so far inland.

For its July missions VIII Bomber Command's loss rate was 5.5 per cent as against RAF Bomber Command's 3.4 per cent. In was known that the Luftwaffe had bolstered its day fighter units in the west by some 200 aircraft, chiefly from the Russian and Italian fronts, during the summer. German fighter tactics had also improved, with greater use of cannon armament and the concentration of interceptions against the more exposed elements of bomber formations. For their part, the Americans experimented with a special gun-platform version of the Fortress designated YB-40, which had no bombs but carried a vast amount of ammunition and had two extra powered turrets giving a total of fourteen guns. The plan was for these aircraft to be positioned on the extremities of a formation and act as escort for the bombers. In practice these proved of little value and too slow to keep up with the bombers on return after they had released their bombs.

While the Eighth Air Force's B-17s slogged it out with the Luftwaffe in western Europe, its B-24 Liberator groups were in North Africa. They were to launch the most daring and undoubtedly the most famous American bomber raid of the war. Oil had been a priority target for RAF Bomber Command in the early days of its attacks on the Reich, only to be neglected when it was deemed that the required precision and weight to effect plant destruction was not available. The USAAF strategists had also identified oil as a major objective, and they regarded it highly vulnerable to air attack. It was estimated that between one-third and a half of Germany's oil requirements were being met from the fields around the Romanian town of Ploesti, where most refineries were situated. The first US strategic bombing raid of the war with Germany had been by a small number of Liberators against Ploesti in June 1942, flying from a base in the Middle East. That night attack was a complete failure and probably did more harm than good by alerting the Germans to the possibility of further attacks and the need for strong defences. Ploesti oil remained an inviting target for the USAAF, however, and in the early summer of 1943 a plan was accepted for a maximum effort by Libera-

Below: On 20/21 April 1943 Stirling BF476/LS:P was one of fifteen No 15 Squadron aircraft that set off from Mildenhall bound for Rostock. Its load was one 1,000lb HE and 270 ∞ 4lb and 40 ∞ 30lb incendiaries. Loss of engine power precipitated a successful crash-landing near Vejle in North Jutland, where Flt Lt C. P. Lyons and crew set fire to the aircraft. (IWM HU20619)

tors, the only type available with the necessary range for a 1,900-mile round trip from North Africa. The three B-24 groups in England were sent down to join the two assigned to the Ninth Air Force in Libya, where a dummy Ploesti oil complex was built in the desert for training purposes. The mission was to be flown at low level to avoid radar detection and, it was hoped, obtain surprise with an approach from the north-

west. The mission was launched on 1 August, a Sunday when the Romanian workers were less likely to be at the plants.

A task force of 179 B-24s was despatched, flying to the coast of Yugoslavia and then across Hungary. During the long flight the two leading groups became separated from the trailing three and on approach to the Ploesti area the leader mistook a small town for the briefed Initial Point and turned for the target too soon. The following groups turned on the correct IP, only to find some of their targets already attacked by B-24s coming from another direction with the defences fully alerted. In the confusion some targets were attacked twice and others not at all. However, the two trailing groups, flying the mission exactly as planned, did some excellent bombing and put the refineries attacked out of action for several months. The cost of this operation was 54 B-24s, underlying yet again the dangers of committing heavy bombers to low-level attack. The many courageous acts this day brought the unprecedented award of five Medals of Honor, the highest US award for bravery.

Before the Eighth Air Force B-24s were returned to England, in the cause of Pointblank, the USAAF devised an ambitious plan for simultaneous attacks on the Messerschmitt plant at Wiener-Neustadt in Austria by these aircraft flying from North Africa and by a force of B-17s from England which

Left: A fusillade of 20mm cannon shells and 7.9mm bullets from a Luftwaffe night fighter was responsible for this damage to Stirling BF517/AA:O of No 75 Squadron on the night of 26/27 April 1943. The rear gunner, Sgt B. A. Rogers, was mortally wounded and two other crew members suffered minor wounds. The pilot, P Off P. J. Buck, managed to evade further attacks when the Stirling was intercepted 30 miles north of the target, Duisburg, but had difficulty in maintaining altitude. Other crew members jettisoned all movable equipment on the flight home, a crash-landing being made at Newmarket without further injury to the airmen. (IWM CE58)
Below: The combat début of the twin-engine Martin B-26 Marauder medium bomber was hardly a

success. Flying at low altitude, a dozen aircraft of the 322nd Bomb Group attacked the generating station at Ijmuiden, Holland, on 14 May 1943. Heavy ground fire was encountered and several of the Marauders were hit. All returned to their Bury St Edmunds base, but B-26B 117988/DR:R was so badly damaged and difficult to control that its pilot, Lt John Howell, ordered the crew to bale out. Before Howell could follow, the Marauder spun into a field at Rougham, with fatal results. Nothing could be done but let the wreckage burn. The target was, apparently, unscathed and three days later eleven 322nd Marauders were sent out again to attack it. One aborted and all the others failed to return. Thereafter no more low-level missions were flown with Marauders. (USAAF)

would attack the Messerschmitt plant at Regensburg and fly on to land in North Africa, a shuttle mission similar to that undertaken by RAF Lancasters in June. The operation was set for 7 August but the fickle European weather forced a cancellation. It was then decided that the Liberators would fly their mission separately, and this was accomplished on 13 August with excellent bombing results and the loss of only two of the 114 despatched. The shuttle mission was still to go ahead at the first opportunity and would be undertaken by the 4th Wing.

To spread the enemy defences, the 1st Wing B-17s flew on a parallel course to attack the ball-bearing plant at Schweinfurt before returning to England.

The weather prognosis being fine for 17 August, the first anniversary of the Eighth's heavy bomber début, 146 Fortresses set off for Regensburg. Unfortunately heavy mist at their more inland airfields, delaying the departure of 230 for Schweinfurt, gave enough time for fighters intercepting the 4th Wing to land, refuel and take off to meet the Schweinfurt force. An

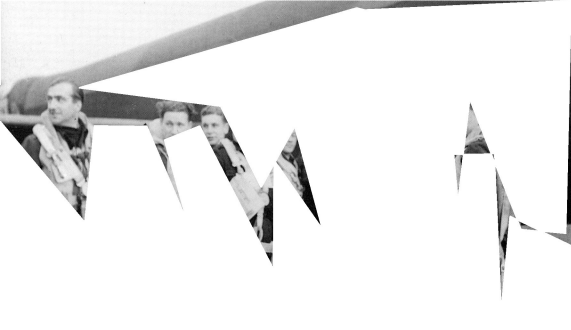

Left, upper: The same day as the Marauders flew their first mission, the American 'heavies' went to strike shipyards at Kiel. A total of 115 Fortresses of the 1st Bomb Wing and 21 Liberators of the 44th Bomb Group were despatched, while 3rd Bomb Wing B-17s attacked targets in the Low Countries as a diversion. The loaded B-24s had proved unable to hold the high altitudes at which the B-17s usually flew and in consequence were more vulnerable to both flak and fighters. This proved to be the case this day, when 44th aircraft, flying some 3,000 to 4,000ft below the B-17s, took heavy punishment. Lt William Cameron (left) and Maj Howard Moore (centre), who had been on leave in London and were too late to take part in the mission, are seen awaiting the return of the Liberators on this bright spring day. Five did not return; one had Moore's crew with another pilot, and Cameron's aircraft was lost with another crew. Moore and Cameron later realised that, of the 90 original aircrew of their squadron, the 67th, that commenced operations in November 1942, they were the only two still assigned. The rest had been lost on operations, killed in accidents or transferred out for health or other reasons. (W.R.Cameron)

Left, lower: The legendary Wg Cdr Guy Gibson, about to enter Lancaster ED932/AJ:G, the aircraft in which he led the famous dams raid of 16/17 May 1943. Gibson later lost his life in a Mosquito crash in the Netherlands; his death did not appear to be due to enemy action. ED932 remained with No 617 Squadron to deliver a number of 12,000lb Tallboys and survived the war. (IWM CH18005)

Right, upper: With No 3 feathered and No 4 throwing oil, B-17F 229793/BO:P of the 368th Bomb Squadron is nursed home across the North Sea by 1/Lt George E. Paris and his co-pilot. At 1257hrs, during the bomb run at Wilhelmshaven on 21 May 1943, the seventeen Fortresses of the 306th Bomb Group formation were attacked by FW 190s. Flying left on the leading B-17, Paris's aircraft sustained 20mm

estimated 300 Luftwaffe fighters were airborne and were responsible for most of the 36 B-17s lost by the 1st Wing and 24 lost by the 4th. Some groups were under almost constant attack and the air battles were without previous equal in intensity. The US gunners claimed 288 enemy fighters shot down, the real figure being 27 although about half probably fell to US fighters. The bombing was particularly accurate at Regensburg, and this force had few interceptions after heading for North Africa. A week later the B-17s returned to Eng-

land, bombing an airfield near Bordeaux en route. Like the RAF, the Eighth Air Force found that problems with making repairs and general servicing at North African bases did not justify repeating missions of this nature.

The 60 bombers missing on one day, from a force of 376, represented a 16 per cent loss rate, but as only 310 aircraft actually attacked the primary targets and seven of those that returned were classified too badly damaged to repair, the percentage rate of loss could be presented as much higher. Day-

cannon shell hits on the right wing and engines. Another hit, on the left side of the radio room, wounded the operator. Three 306th B-17s were lost as a result of enemy fighter attacks, one ditching and its crew being rescued by a Royal Navy minesweeper. VIII Bomber Command lost 11 per cent of its force bombing Wilhelmshaven that day—no wonder that, during the first half of 1943, a bomber crewman had less than a one-in-three chance of completing his tour of 25 missions. (USAAF)

Right, lower: Mosquito bombers carried out several successful far-ranging daylight attacks in the year preceding No 2 Group's removal from Bomber Command on 1 June 1943. The unarmed aircraft relied on their speed and surprise to survive the enemy defences, flying at low level and usually attacking at dusk. The last and most daring mission by the two squadrons, Nos 105 and 139, was flown a few days before their transfer to No 8 Pathfinder Group. The optical glass and instrument plants at Jena were the targets, entailing a round trip of over 800 miles. Six aircraft of No 139, led by the CO Wg Cdr Reynolds, were briefed to attack the Schott and Genosseu glass factory and eight from No 105, led by Sqn Ldr Blessing, went for the Zeiss instrument works. Soon after the aircraft had penetrated the Dutch coast, low cloud and poor visibility was encountered and two Mosquitos were lost in a collision while another had to seek a target of opportunity when an engine failed. Despite the atrocious weather, the targets were reached and reported as accurately bombed. The photograph shows No 105 Mosquitos preparing to take off from Marham at 1920hrs. The aircraft in the foreground, DZ467/GB:P, flown by P Off Massie, was the only No 105 Squadron aircraft failing to return. Two other aircraft, one from each squadron, crashed on return, one while trying to land at Coltishall and the other at home base. Both crews were killed. (IWM CH18012)

light precision bombing was causing serious damage and the cost would have been justified if production had been terminated. But the fact was that, even where production had been stopped or curtailed, it was usually back to near normal within a few weeks. The powers of the enemy's recuperation were much underestimated and, as the RAF had found, it was necessary to return again and again to a target. The Germans, fully realising the dangers of the mounting bomber offensive, were busy dispersing production to minimise the effects of the loss of any one source.

VIII Bomber Command was forced to lick its wounds and regain strength before any further deep penetrations of enemy airspace, and at such times the weather fronts that usually dogged its efforts were almost welcome. RAF Bomber Command's percentage losses were nearing 5 per cent in August as it too confronted increasingly effective enemy defences. On the night following the Eighth Air Force's African shuttle, almost 600 'heavies' were sent to make a precision attack on the experimental weapons site at Peenemünde. The bombing destroyed many facilities but had no great effect on the V-weapon

Left: Mosquito crewmen Sqn Ldr V. R. G. Harcourt DFC and W Off J. Friendly DFM, of No 139 Squadron, being interrogated at RAF Marham in May 1943.(IWM CH18007)

Left: Much was made of United States volunteers who served in the RAF's Eagle fighter squadrons, yet far more airmen of that nation flew with other commands. Fg Off Fisher, who took part in the 27 May 1943 venture, called his No 105 Squadron Mosquito DK337/GB:H *Uncle Sam*. The thirteenth raid, to Berlin, has special acknowledgement. Many US nationals transferred to the USAAF in 1943 but others preferred to stay with the RAF. (IWM CH10114)

development programme apart from killing several important members of the staff, including the director. The venture cost 40 bombers missing in action.

Harris began to look towards Berlin as the target where his strengthened forces would be most likely to break the enemy's morale. On the night of 23/24 August he sent 727 bombers to the German capital and the loss nearly equalled that of the Eighth Air Force's shuttle mission. Of the 56 aircraft missing in action, 23 were Halifaxes and sixteen Stirlings, with loss-to-sortie rates of 9.2 and 13 per cent respectively, whereas the Lancasters were at 4.9 per cent. This was a worrying trend for the slower, lower types, the Stirling's operational ceiling being only 10,000 to 14,000ft. The weather had been poor and the bombing scattered. On the last night of the month RAF Bomber Command tried again with a hundred fewer bombers, only to suffer similar cruel losses with the Stirling's rate even higher at 16 per cent. Since the introduction of Window the bombers were despatched in type waves so that the Window dispensed by the higher flying Lancasters would aid the Halifaxes and Stirlings. However, this left the slower Stirlings at the mercy of night fighter concentration on the return flight. Lancasters had taken the long haul to Berlin on 3/4 September for a 6.9 per cent loss rate, also deemed too high for continuing attacks. Berlin was left alone for a few weeks while Bomber Command reviewed tactics.

The Dortmund–Ems Canal, an old favourite on Bomber Command's target list, came to the fore again early in September in tragic circumstances. The special Lancaster squadron which had carried out the dams raid in May attempted a low-level moonlight breaching of this waterway with 12,000lb bombs, only to fail and lose five of the eight aircraft sent.

Some of the crews were those who had survived the dams raid. Once more the dangers of operating big bombers at low level were restated.

In October 1943 new countermeasure devices were introduced. ABC, also known as Airborne Cigar, consisted of transmitting equipment which a German-speaking operator used to jam the verbal radio communications of night fighter crews. The aircraft with this capability were dispersed along the bomber stream and the employment of ABC undoubtedly limited interceptions. Similar jamming of the German raid controller broadcasts were carried out from the UK by a system called Corona, which also proved effective. Yet, for all these endeavours to fox the night fighters, the rule of thumb was that the deeper the bombers penetrated, the higher would be the losses. RAF Bomber Command's best work continued to be at targets within Oboe range, although H2S pathfinding was improving. At Kassel on 22/23 October both target-marking and main force bombing was precise enough to bring that unfortunate city its most devastating night of the war. The destruction is said to have been akin to that at Hamburg, and the total death toll ran to some 6,000 souls.

October 1943 was a crucial month for the US Eighth Air Force. The one major effort in September, against Stuttgart's industry, was totally foiled by cloud and 45 B-17s were lost, several running out of fuel and going down in the Channel. Cloud restricted attacks to targets in occupied France for most of the month so, when early October promised clearer skies, Eaker was determined to take full advantage and press Pointblank aims. A force of 104 B-17s was sent to aircraft industry targets at Frankfurt and Wiesbaden, while 51 more had Frankfurt city as their primary target on 4 October. An-

Right: Flying was always a risky business without enemy action. A sudden engine failure precipitated the crash of this Mosquito coming in to land, and the aircraft was immediately engulfed in flames. Nothing could be done for the crew. To see men survive all the enemy could throw at them only to 'get the chop' in an accident was always a morale-sapping occasion. There was little the padre could do on this occasion as a rescue crew try to remove remains. (IWM CH18732)

Left, upper: Ground crews cycle along the Alconbury perimeter track bound for the mess hall on a bright day in May 1943. The nearest aircraft is YB-40 25745/UX:H of the 327th Bomb Squadron, the only unit to be equipped with this type. Fitted with an extra top turret, the first nose 'chin turret' and extra guns in the waist positions, the type was intended to act as a flying dreadnought to protect other Fortresses. It was not a success,

being heavy, slow and just as vulnerable to fighter attack as standard B-17s. The far Fortress is a B-17F, 23165/NV:G of the 325th Bomb Squadron. It was shot down by flak on 26 November 1943, seven of the crew being killed and three made POWs. (IWM D15131)
Left, lower: Pocklington, 19 June 1943: Halifax II DT743/DY:O, with Sgt T. H. Dargavel at the controls, begins its take-off run in the gathering gloom. Airmen spectators

watch, give the thumbs up and wave the bomber off with a wish of good luck. None of the 23 No 102 Squadron Halifaxes bound for Le Creusot that night were lost. The Schneider works was one of the largest armament factories in France and its output of considerable value to the Germans. The factory was hit, but the bombing was not concentrated and casualties among the local French did little to enhance the RAF's reputation. (IWM CH10331)

Above: Flt Lt J. A.Wakeford entering Lancaster ED689/WS:K of No 9 Squadron for his fiftieth operation at Bardney, 20 June 1943. The target was Friedrichshafen, and after bombing the Lancasters landed at Bilda in North Africa, returning two nights later and attacking Spezia en route. On 3/4 July 1943 'luck ran out' for the Wakeford crew and the same Lancaster when they were the only loss of the Squadron in a raid on Cologne. (IWM CH10404)

other 206 US 'heavies' were out this day and total losses amounted to sixteen. On the 8th clear sky forecasts over northwest Germany saw 399 bombers sent to Bremen and Vegesack, with strong fighter opposition to all elements bringing a loss of 30. The Baltic coast area was the destination for 378 heavy bombers next day, with spectacular bombing results at the Marienburg fighter factory and little opposition to the 3rd Bomb Division (previously 4th Wing). It was a different story at Anklem, where the 1st Bomb Division attacked another aviation plant: fighter interceptions were largely responsible for bringing down eighteen B-17s, 15.7 per cent of the force briefed for that target. Total losses for the day were 28 'heavies' and, on the morrow, 30 when VIII Bomber Command went out for the third day running. All but one of this number

fell from the 3rd Division formations, totalling 133 B-17s—a 22.6 per cent loss. Worse was to come. Four days later the Eighth Air Force despatched both B-17 divisions in an attempt to finish off the Schweinfurt factories, the major source of ball-bearing production in the Reich, where destruction could affect the construction of aircraft and fighting vehicles. The target, 250 miles from the Channel coast, was expected to be heavily contested, and so it proved.

Some 400 enemy fighters were airborne that day, and the bombers attacked with few breaks during both penetration and withdrawal. Of 291 B-17s despatched, 229 bombed and 60 failed to return, a 20.6 per cent loss. VIII Bomber Command's loss rate for October 1943 worked out at 9.2 per cent, and as 10 per cent was the advised limit beyond which casualties

Left, upper: One of the most successful VIII Bomber Command attacks during the early summer of 1943 was the mission to the synthetic rubber plant at Hüls, which was also the first major bombing of a Ruhr target by the Eighth Air Force. A good concentration of strikes on the plant resulted in a pall of black smoke rising high above the town and making accurate aim difficult for the last formations in the task force. Despite extensive damage, production was under way again within a few weeks, an example of the Germans' well-organised repair operations. In this view B-17F 23051/KY:M, *Hells Angels*, of the 366th Bomb Squadron, 305th Bomb Group, is on its bomb run amid flak. The 305th Group was originally commanded by Col Curtis LeMay, who was responsible for a number of tactical developments in daylight bombing. (IWM US88)

Left, lower: At Hüls the leading 91st Bomb Group took the brunt of an enemy fighter assault with many frontal attacks, five of its Fortresses failing to return. Lt Buster Peek and his men in 229797/LL:Y, *Old Ironsides*, managed to regain the Channel and ditch. All escaped from the aircraft, but the tail gunner disappeared. An RAF air–sea rescue craft picked up the nine survivors within half an hour and gave emergency dressings to three who had been wounded in the air battle. Their wet clothing was temporarily replaced with RAF uniforms, which were still being worn by the wounded men when they were visited in hospital by the Group CO, Lt-Col Baskin Lawrence. Standing behind Lawrence is the bombardier, Lt Chauncy Hicks; in bed is T/Sgt James F. Osborne, radio operator; and sitting on the bed is S/Sgt William G. Zeigler, a gunner. RAF ASR had plucked several hundred US airmen from the sea by the end of the war. (USAAF)

should no longer be sustained, a crisis situation held sway at Eaker's HQ. Recovery of numbers took time, and in any case the weather precluded major operations for some weeks. While VIII Bomber Command was henceforth more cautious in exposing its bomber formations to such risk without good cause, there was never any directive to curtail the unescorted day missions. If weather opportunity had allowed attacks on important Pointblank targets, Eaker would have despatched his force.

Balanced against these losses were some very good bombing results, notwithstanding the fact that at the time they were not as effective as then believed. The bomber gunners had claims of 186 enemy fighters shot down on the 14th and many more probable and damage claims. Here, too, although exaggeration was appreciated, the USAAF authorities thought a heavy toll was being exacted from the Luftwaffe. At long last the new groups Eaker wanted were scheduled to arrive at a faster rate and, as RAF Bomber Command operations had

shown, the larger the force the more likely the percentage loss rate could be contained. But the most promising turn was the provision and success of long-range fighter escort. In April 1943 three groups of P-47 Thunderbolt fighters had commenced supporting the day bomber missions. Their radius of action was initially limited to some 200 miles from base. In late July the introduction of jettisionable fuel tanks enabled the Thunderbolts to fly as far as the German border and the provision of a pressurised tank the following month permitted flights as far as Emden and the Ruhr. Moreover, the heavy P-47, which was originally thought a poor match to the enemy's Me 109s and FW 190s, was being used with great skill and success—so much so that the Luftwaffe now staged its main assaults on the US bombers over the Reich beyond the range of the Thunderbolts. The first two groups of P-38 Lightnings, with even greater range, had arrived. It was to the fighters that Eighth Air Force now looked to save its day bomber assaults.

Right: Cpt Frank D. Yaussi checks the 500lb GPs in a B-17 at Bassingbourn, 30 June 1943. As the 306th Bomb Group's lead bombardier, Yaussi was the first Eighth Air Force man to drop bombs on Germany, on 27 January 1943. He later became the Combat Wing lead bombardier. (USAAF)

Right: Unfused, TNT or Amatol bombs did not pose a great threat in handling and it was usual for them to be unloaded from trucks in this fashion, the paper composition rings having a cushioning effect. RDX-filled bombs were not so stable and there were serious accidents, including the almost complete destruction of one airfield bomb dump in Suffolk. These armourers are busy with 500lb M-43s at Chelveston, 29 June 1943. (USAAF)

Right: Surviving two operational tours during the early years of RAF Bomber Command operations was considered long odds. Survivors were looked upon with some awe by the more pessimistic. No 196 Squadron had this team of veterans who finished up on 28/29 June 1943. Left to right are W Off T. E. Mellor, pilot, a former accountant from Derby, aged 25 and with 29 trips of a first tour; Flt Sgt H. G. Webb, bomb-aimer, a former clerk from Market Harborough, aged 23 and with 54 trips; W Off L. W. Quick, navigator, a former shop assistant from Taunton, aged 23 and with 54 trips; Flt Sgt J. Alison, rear gunner, a former glass worker from Chelmsford, aged 23 and with 51 trips; and Flt Sgt R. Williamson, wireless operator, a former shop assistant from Darlington, aged 21 and with 46 trips. No 196 Squadron had a fairly brief life as a Bomber Command squadron, a matter of ten months in 1943 before being transferred to airborne forces support shortly after converting to Stirlings. For five months Wellington Xs were flown from Leconfield with No 4 Group, where this photograph was taken. (IWM CH10255)

Above: A few days after this photograph of a Halifax II, JD206/DY:T, was taken at Pocklington, Flt Sgt G. S. Honey and crew set off in it bound for Mulheim, the raid of 22/23 June 1943. On the way in, while flying over Oberflakke, the bomber was hit by flak (!). Three engines were put out of action and, with only the starboard outer running, Honey had to put the aircraft into a dive to avoid stalling. As parachuting into the sea was not the best option, after jettisoning the bomb load Honey elected to ditch. This was accomplished successfully in the bright moonlight and the crew took to the dinghy. At first light a drogue was raised and was seen by low-flying Mustangs at 0625hrs. Later in the day Typhoons flew over and eventually two No 277 Squadron Walrus amphibians arrived. One boarded Honey and another member of the crew and took off for Martlesham. The other Walrus, too heavily loaded, was unable to become airborne and proceeded to taxi towards England. The situation was relieved when the Halifax crew were transferred to a motor gunboat from Felixstowe. (IWM CH10776)

Below: The hostile environment to which they were committed came as a shock to the personnel of the new B-17 groups joining the Eighth Air Force in the early summer of 1943. The effectiveness of the enemy defences and the frequent poor flying conditions were not appreciated until experienced. Typical was the 379th Bomb Group, which for its fifth mission was sent to Hamburg on 25 June 1943, only to become disorganised in heavy cloud and persistent contrails to such an extent that it never reached its objective and had to attack a target of opportunity. Intercepted by fighters, six of its twenty Fortresses were shot down and several others badly damaged. One of the losses was the 526th Bomb Squadron's 42-30107/LF:D, *Black Magic*, which crashed at Wieste, west of Cloppenburg, at 0910hrs. Two of Lt Weldon Homes' crew were killed and eight made prisoner. (IWM HU25811)

Above: The number of bombers lost to bombs dropped from higher aircraft on night raids was never established, although a score of such incidents are known. Flt Sgt D. Cameron's Halifax, HR837/NP:F of No 158 Squadron, was 'clobbered' over Cologne on 28/29 June 1943. It is seen here at home station Lissett the following day. (IWM CE84)
Left: Wg Cdr A. E. Lowe MBE DFC started out as an air gunner with Bomber Command and eventually rose to become a squadron commander. (IWM CH10564)

Right: For crews brought down over France or the Low Countries there was often a good chance of evading capture and being returned to Britain by one of the clandestine escape organisations operated by brave people who would most likely be executed if apprehended with Allied airmen. When the 412th Bomb Squadron's 230105/QW:R, *Slightly Dangerous*, was crippled during a fighter attack on a cloud-frustrated mission to Le Bourget airfield on 10 July 1943, four members of the crew were able to bale out before the aircraft crashed at St Didier des Bois, Normandy. The engineer and right waist gunner were taken prisoner, but co-pilot R. M. McGowen and radio operator D. E. Harding managed to evade and were befriended by local French people. Early in this month the heavy bomber groups of VIII Bomber Command began to display an identifying marking on the vertical tail surfaces. The 1st Wing used a triangle device, the 2nd Wing a circle and the 4th a square. The letter within the device varied from group to group; square B was that of the 95th Bomb Group. (S. Blandin)

Below: Henry Stimson, US Secretary of War, reads the citation before decorating S/Sgt Maynard Smith with the Medal of Honor, the highest US award of gallantry. 'Snuffy' Smith was the first Eighth Air Force recipient, although a posthumous award had been made for an earlier action. A total of fourteen Medal of Honor awards were made to Eighth Air Force fliers and those participating in its operations by the end of hostilities, half of all to members of the USAAF. Smith was ball turret gunner on a 306th Bomb Group which took fire in the radio room after being shot up on the St Nazaire mission of 1 May. After other crew members in the rear of the aircraft baled out, Smith fought the fire, eventually extinguishing it and enabling a safe landing to be made in Cornwall. The ceremony took place at Thurleigh on 15 July 1943. (USAAF)

Right: 'The guys running the show': ACM Sir Arthur Harris, C-in-C RAF Bomber Command, and Maj-Gen Ira Eaker, Eighth Air Force Commanding General, take the salute at an awards ceremony at Bushy Park, Teddington, 17 July 1943. Despite different views on the execution of the strategic bombing campaign, they remained lifelong friends. (USAAF)

Left: At 04.26hrs on 26 July 1943 Flt Lt C.M.Shannon crash-landed Halifax V Series I (Special) DK148/MP:<u>G</u> at Holme-on-Spalding Moor. On approach to Essen the port inner engine appeared to have been damaged by shrapnel as vibration set in. Shortly after bombing, at 17,000ft, the propeller on the port inner became uncontrollable, eventually separating from the engine and slashing into the aircraft's nose. The impact caused a loss of control and when Shannon brought *Johnnie the Wolf* back to level flight it was discovered that the mid-upper gunner had baled out. The broken wooden propeller blades lessened engine damage but in this case the damage sustained in flight, plus that of the crash-landing, rendered the Halifax a write-off. Two weeks later Shannon and crew failed to return from another target. (IWM CE91)

Right: Public subscription to the cost of specific items of war equipment was given official encouragement by most combatant nations. The First World War veterans of the Salonika Reunion Association in Britain bought a 4,000lb 'Cookie' for delivery to a German target. The missile is here seen before loading in *Hellzapoppin* of No 61 Squadron at Syerston. This Lancaster was a veteran of 71 sorties at the time. (IWM CE109)

Left: A 98th Bomb Group Liberator at smokestack height over the Astro Romana refinery, Ploesti, 1 August 1943. This, its briefed target, had already been attacked by an errant formation. The 98th suffered the highest losses of all five participating groups, nineteen of the 48 despatched. A unique mission in many respects, it is probably the most famous American bombing operation of the Second World War. (Mike Bailey)

Left: The morning after: a raid participant inspects the damage to a 98th Bomb Group B-24D at Benina Main, Libya, after the low-level Ploesti mission. The damage was probably caused by 20mm ground fire. (W.R.Cameron)

Above: The rural surroundings of bomber stations meant that farming activities continued close to those of war. Long grass could be a fire hazard but to a farmer it was useful fodder. Here late hay is taken beside an Elvington dispersal in mid-July, where Halifax II DT807/KN:R *Rita* of No 77 Squadron has the attention of its ground crew. This bomber was lost on its 32nd sortie, on 3/4 October 1943 during the Kassel raid. (IWM CH10598)

Right: Pursued by an FW 190, a vanquished Fortress—believed one of five lost by the 384th Bomb Group—begins its descent to earth 20,000ft below during the Schweinfurt mission, 17 August 1943. (USAAF, 25626AC)

Left: The Messerschmitt factory at Regensburg under a cloud of smoke, midday on 17 August 1943, photographed from a Fortress of the 385th Bomb Group as it began the long flight to North Africa. (USAAF)

Below: The wing of the 551st Bomb Squadron's 23290/R *Raunchy Wolf* provides shade from the fierce African sun. Aircrew had to perform their own maintenance before the flight back to England, attacking a target in France en route. This B-17F was lost in a collision over south-east Essex while returning from a mission on 26 September 1943. Only one gunner survived of the twenty aircrew involved. (USAAF)

Right: The rocket and flying bomb experimental station at Peenemünde on 17/18 August 1943. The photograph was taken from a Lancaster, catching two other Lancasters at a lower level and illustrating how, during a concentrated attack, lower-flying aircraft could be struck by bombs from those at higher altitude. (IWM C3748)

Below: A Lancaster that had a lucky escape on the 17/18 August 1943 Peenemünde mission was ED611/KM:J of No 44 Squadron, captained by P Off D. H. Aldridge. The aircraft was shot up on the starboard side and the outer engine was damaged, as was the right undercarriage assembly. The turret hydraulics were also shot out. Aldridge was able successfully to bring the bomber down at base even though the right tyre had burst. The crew were all safe. ED611 was repaired and later, after major overhaul, sent to No 463 Squadron. The holes in the fuselage were made by 20mm shells. The roundel marking of British service aircraft was changed in mid-1942 to the form shown with reduced white to avoid compromising camouflage. (IWM CH10917)

Above left: The flak at Flushing was not rated a major hazard but even a small anti-aircraft battery could put up accurate fire four miles high. One moment B-17F 229807/WF:O, *Liberty Lady*, of the 364th Bomb Squadron, was untroubled, the next a direct hit had severed its fuselage just aft of the radio room. There seemed little hope for Lt Ralph Miller's crew as the stricken machine fell towards the sea, but two men were able to parachute and were rescued by the Germans. (USAAF)

Above right: The 6 September 1943 mission to bomb industrial targets at Stuttgart ranks as the most fruitless large-scale operation ever undertaken by the Eighth Air Force. Extensive cloud foiled accurate bombing and dispersed the task force, which mostly attacked targets of opportunity. The cost was 333 men missing in action from the 45 B-17s failing to return and two dead and 27 wounded in those that did. Over a hundred B-17s returning had some form of battle damage and there were nine write-offs in crash-landings. The crashes and at least a dozen of the losses were caused by many of the older aircraft running out of fuel. Capt Jacob James managed to get 229944/GN:E, *Winning Run*, of the 427th Bomb Squadron, in sight of the small RAF airfield at Deanland near the South Coast cliffs, only to have the engines fail on approach. All walked away from the crash-landing. Here one survivor watches another B-17 low on fuel going into land. (USAAF)

Left: The youngest squadron commander in Bomber Command was Wg Cdr C. H. Baigent DFC and Bar, a 21-year-old from New Zealand. He took over No 75 (NZ) Squadron early in 1944 and remained in command for a year. (IWM CH14676)

Right, upper: An Australian 'Gen' crew of No 466 Squadron who completed their tour on 30/31 August 1943, the penultimate operation before the squadron was stood down to convert from Wellingtons to Halifaxes. The last of five Royal Australian Air Force heavy bomber squadrons to become operational with Bomber Command, No 466 served as part of No 4 Group. Unlike the RCAF, the RAAF did not have its own group and the Australian-manned squadrons were spread among the other groups. Standing before 'their' Wellington, HE984/HD:H *Snifter*, with its insignia of Hitler, Mussolini, Göring and Goebbels confronted by a canine puddle, are Flt Sgt J. P. Hetherington (bomb-aimer), P Off J. H. Cameron (pilot), P Off J. J. Allen (navigator), Flt Sgt J. Samuels (WO/AG) and P Off A. C. Winston (rear gunner). Nose armament had been discarded at this stage in the war and the turret sealed. (IWM CH11173)

Right, lower: Tea and a puff of Navy Cut ease weary men: Flt Sgt S. Mason and his crew at interrogation following the 23/24 August 1943 trip to Berlin. No 90 Squadron at Wratting Common detailed twenty Stirlings for this raid and two failed to return. Mason captained EH906/WP:T and a few minutes after midnight he was serenaded on the intercom with 'Happy Birthday'; it was his twenty-first. EH906 was lost on its 39th sortie on 5 March 1944, a special duties operation dropping equipment to the French Resistance. The standard-issue whistle attached to the jacket collar of the sergeant on the right was for seeking help if injured in a crash or a parachute landing. (IWM CH10804)

Above: One of the 56 RAF Bomber Command aircraft that failed to return from the preliminary round of the Battle of Berlin on 23/24 August 1943 was Halifax JD379/KN:M from No 77 Squadron, flown by Flt Sgt A. Massie and crew. Hit by flak, the bomber came down at Quelch, north of Celle. (IWM HU25822)

Below: No 51 Squadron Halifax II Series I HR782/MH:V, with Fg Off R. Burchett and crew, successfully carried out an attack on München-Gladbach during the night of 29/30 August 1943, with few problems until returning to England. At 0403hrs, while at 4,000ft ten miles south-east of their Ossington base, there was a collision with a Lancaster, thought to be on a reciprocal course. The top of the port fin was knocked off and both port propellers were damaged. Burchett could only keep control by increasing speed, but he managed successfully to bring the aircraft down at 180mph. As so often happened, following repair the aircraft was finally lost at a later date—in this case after 168 hours' total flying time on the Leipzig raid of 3/4 December 1943. (IWM CE97)

Left: By the autumn of 1943 the Lancaster had become the major type in RAF Bomber Command. No 207 Squadron was one of the first with Lancasters but was unfortunate in suffering some of the highest losses and in Nissen-hut rumour was a 'chop' squadron. LM326/EM:Z lasted four months before failing to return from the Hanover raid of 18/19 October 1943 with Flt Sgt G.Taylor and crew. Photographed on a local flight, it is seen here against a background of countryside east of Grantham. Prominent is Barkston Heath airfield, recently brought up to Class A standard for a bomber airfield. Typical of the type, it had three intersecting concrete runways, dispersals for 50 aircraft and accomodation for some 2,500 personnel. The cost of such an airfield was £1,000,000. (IWM CH12115)

Below: Most RAF Bomber Command stations had a WAAF site whose occupants performed a variety of duties ranging through domestic, secretarial, maintenance and vehicle driving. The bomb trains were often collected and delivered by WAAFs. This young woman is using a David Brown tractor at East Kirkby's bomb dump circa November 1943. The 'B 5' on the mudguard denotes Bomber Command No 5 Group.(IWM CH18359)

Above: A Halifax of No 1663 Heavy Conversion Unit makes its approach to Rufforth airfield over off-duty WAAFs at play. There were a score of HCUs under RAF Bomber Command control and each usually had a complement of more than 30 aircraft. The purpose of these units was to take trainee crews from OTUs and give them an introduction to the bomber type they would fly with the operational squadrons. The aircraft employed by HCUs were mostly worn veterans of combat, which may have played a part in the high accident rate suffered by these units. HCUs were occasionally called upon to supply crews and aircraft for operations, although this rarely occurred after 1943. (IWM CH11531)

Below: The need for more destructive power in one missile resulted in the 12,000lb bomb, made by bolting together three 4,000lb sections and adding a tail unit. Such bombs were first used on 15/16 September in the disastrous attempt by No 617 Squadron to breach the Dortmund–Ems Canal. Modifications necessary to enable Lancasters to carry this weapon were first effected on No 617's aircraft and included the removal of the nose and mid-upper turrets to reduce weight. The new weapon in this photograph is displayed before a No 617 Lancaster at Scampton. The marking '51/40/9' on the bomb was the reference to the explosive filling, which could be Armatex, RDX/TNT or Torpex 2. (IWM CH12454)

Left: Twice in the latter half of 1943 the Eighth Air Force's B-24 groups were sent to assist in the Mediterranean campaigns, joining the two B-24 groups of that theatre on operations, where the controlling command was the Twelfth Air Force. Facilities at Tunisian airfields were often basic and maintenance had to performed in the open, where dry summer conditions made dust a hazard in contrast to the frequent damp of England. Heat and dust were the common lot of the two resident Liberator groups, which made engine changing, as on this 98th Bomb Group aircraft, an exacting task. Keeping abrasive grit out of engines and other sensitive equipment was both difficult and time-consuming. (USAAF)

Below: A salvo release of ten 500lb GP M-43s over Emden on 2 October 1943. The ball turret guns are facing forward as the gunner on Lt K. S. Knowlton's crew checks that all bombs have released—standard operating procedure when not under attack. Sticking bomb shackles were not uncommon in severe icing conditions. An early combat B-17F of the 335th Bomb Squadron, 95th Bomb Group, 230172/OE:S *Darlin' Dolly* eluded most of what the Luftwaffe threw at it, to be retired and eventually modified to carry 20,000lb of explosives as a radio-controlled flying bomb. It was launched at Oldenburg on 1 January 1945, the last operation of the Aphrodite Project. (USAF. 25623)

Right: Using detachable wing shackles, the bomb load of B-17s could be substantially increased for short-range missions. However, altitude capability was also reduced, and apart from a few operations in the second half of 1943 these shackles were rarely used. These 2,000lb M-34s are about to be loaded on the 549th Bomb Squadron's 230251/T, alias *Piccadilly Queen*, which was lost on the mission of 29 January 1944. Four of the crew survived as POWs. (USAAF)

Below: October 1943 was the crisis month for the Eighth Air Force's self-defending daylight bomber missions, when in five missions 164 bombers were missing and more than 700 damaged, fourteen beyond economical repair. On 8 October, when 30 were lost, the 306th Bomb Group bombed Bremen and came under persistent fighter attack both before and after bombing. Three of its Fortresses went down, 42-5855/RD:T of the 423rd Bomb Squadron with two engines on fire. Lt Dean Rodman and five of his crew survived, although eight parachutes were reported. The bomber crashed at Goldenstedt. (IWM HU25834)

Above: Air battle over Bremen, 8 October 1943: an FW 190 dives away after a frontal pass at the 95th Bomb Group formation. Sixteen of the group's Fortresses sustained battle damage, mostly minor, but aircraft had to crash-land on return to England. The 95th lost no aircraft, while its gunners made claims for 24 of the enemy. It is possible one fighter did fall to the defensive fire of this formation: two dozen is probably greater than the number of attackers involved. (USAAF 25935AC)

Right: The 305th Bomb Group suffered its blackest day on the Eighth's second mission to strike the Schweinfurt bearing factories, 14 October 1943. From one of the leading formations, sixteen B-17Fs were lost to a concentrated assault by Luftwaffe fighters before the target was reached. Despite the fact that his group had been decimated, Lt Joseph Pellegrini, a first generation Italian-American and the lead bombardier that day, persisted in his determination to drop on the assigned aiming point. Pellegrini's skill at the bomb sight earned him the position of Group Bombardier. The photograph was taken after he had completed his 25-mission tour later in the year. (USAAF)

6

THE BATTERING
OF BERLIN

'We can wreck Berlin from end to end if the USAAF will come in on it. It will cost between 400–500 aircraft. It will cost Germany the war.' When wishing to have their way, commanders are apt to exaggerate the prowess of their forces to superiors. Thus Air Chief Marshal Harris's famous statement in a letter to the Prime Minister may be understood. And at the time, November 1943, there is no doubt that RAF Bomber Command's leader did believe that the strategic air forces could still be the principal means of bringing about the demise of Hitler's regime. Laying waste the enemy capital with its built-up area of some 18,000 acres and four million inhabitants was seen as the key to this objective.

The two major strikes at Berlin in August had proved costly, with the highest losses to sorties among the Stirlings and Halifaxes, whose operational ceilings were around 14,000ft and 18,000ft respectively. Consideration was given to restricting these types to shorter penetrations of hostile airspace as more Lancaster-equipped squadrons joined the fray. No 3 Group had already begun the conversion from Stirlings to Lancasters, but it would be several months before it shed the last of the lumbering Shorts. The vices of the Merlin-powered Halifaxes had not helped the record of this type, but the Mk III model, with Hercules radials, had a redeeming performance and was sought as a replacement.

It was the Lancasters with the usual Mosquito pathfinders that went to Berlin on 18/19 November, the 'heavies' losing nine of the 440 despatched. Four nights later the Halifax and Stirling squadrons were included in what was the biggest show of strength against Berlin so far—764 bombers despatched. The raid brought widespread damage and heavy casualties to the Germany capital and an outcry against the 'Terror Fliers'.

This was the last time Stirlings bombed Berlin; five were lost, representing 10 per cent of those sent. A smaller force, predominantly Lancasters, was sent to the same target the next night and the 'heavies' continuing the campaign on 26/27 November were all Lancasters. On these raids losses ran at just over 5 and 6 per cent of sorties, although poor weather over eastern England involved several returning aircraft in crashes when trying to locate their airfields. The night fighters

Right: A number of B-17s and B-24s were lost through the inability of the pilots to feather propellers on failed engines. The degree to which this was occurring over enemy territory was not fully apparent for some months. If sump oil was suddenly lost, the pitch of the propeller blade could not be altered, causing the propeller to 'windmill', setting up extreme vibration and threatening the security of the whole aircraft. Eventually the friction created in the drive gears would cause the propeller to break away. This 390th Bomb Group B-17F experienced this problem with No 1 engine during the 20 October 1943 mission to Duren. Fortunately the crew were able to bring the bomber back to home base at Framlingham, drawing a small crowd to view the damage. (USAAF)

were able to exact a far larger toll on the night of 2/3 December when 40 bombers failed to return from a far from concentrated attack on the city. Equipment failures, inclement weather, enemy decoys and other factors adversely affected the concentration of Bomber Command raids on many occasions, the farther the target the more likely the spread of the bombing—and this held true of Berlin.

Above: A 93rd Bomb Group B-24D takes off from Hardwick for the mission to Wilhelmshaven, 3 November 1943. By late October 1943 the Eighth Air Forces Liberator groups had finished their wanderings and joined the main assault from England. During the winter of 1943–44 most of the new bomb groups arriving in both the ETO and MTO were equipped with Liberators. (USAAF)

The mounting success of the Luftwaffe night fighters led to the formation of a special countermeasures group early in November 1943. With its main concentration in north Norfolk, No 100 Group gathered a variety of units with a mission to support bomber operations through action against the enemy defences. This included the use of airborne radio- and radar-jamming equipment, intruder attacks on enemy night fighter airfields and patrols along the bomber routes by Beaufighters and Mosquitos equipped with devices to home in on enemy night fighter radar. These last-named sorties, known as Serrate, were first undertaken on the night of 16/17 December when yet another Berlin raid was under way. This was a particularly notorious operation, for the ground-hugging cloud over north-east England provoked 29 Lancaster crashes when the bombers returned, more than the 25 missing in action.

Berlin was the main target on two more occasions in 1943 and the two opening nights of 1944. For every raid on this main objective, RAF Bomber Command struck at two other targets and losses were often as high to the ever strengthening defences. At Leipzig on 3/4 December areas of the city had been devastated, with very heavy disruption to Junkers aircraft production using the former Leipzig World Fair buildings.

It was the Americans who were principally involved in meeting the intermediate objective of Combined Bomber Offensive—the neutralisation of the enemy air force—through attacks on the aircraft industry. For a time the winter weather restricted them to targets where H2S and the more reliable US-made version, H2X, could be used to distinguish targets through the cloud. The intention was still to bomb visually, resorting to radar releases only if the target were obscured. When this occurred the Eighth Air Force was indulging in area attack by default, and this was often the case during the winter of 1943–44. For this reason many missions were to locations where a good water/land contrast would be obtained on the radar scopes, Emden, Bremen and Kiel being prominent. These were also targets within escorting fighter range.

The principal staff officers of the Eighth Air Force fighter technical section, through association with the Lockheed P-38 Lightning's first movement to the UK, considered this fighter to be the answer to long-range escort. Unfortunately, although a fine aircraft to fly and an excellent gun platform, the P-38 was dogged with problems, the most critical being engine failure as a result of the low temperatures and humidity encountered at high altitudes over north-west Europe. Engine failure, directly and indirectly, is said to have been the major cause of P-38 losses during the first few weeks of operations. There were, however, American champions of a development of a US fighter originally designed and built by the North American company for the British, the P-51 Mustang. Because of its origins, the USAAF at first tended to have limited interest in the type, and then only for employment in tactical reconnais-

sance, for which the RAF had used those it had put into service in 1942. Experiments with replacing the low-altitude-rated Allison engine with a Merlin resulted in North American producing the P-51B with a Packard-built version of the Merlin. The aircraft had a performance superior in most respects to that of the two main Luftwaffe fighters and, most significantly, a range double that of either the P-38's or the P-47's on internal tankage. Despite these advantages, it was still seen as a tactical fighter by Materiel Command in the United States and initial production was assigned to the Ninth Air Force. Once Eighth Air Force commanders were apprised of the fighter's potential, there was considerable pressure to have all P-51Bs reassigned and the first group with the type to reach the Ninth Air Force was immediately placed under VIII Fighter Command operational control. The group became operational on 1 December.

Disappointment with the rate of operations of VIII Bomber Command had led General Arnold to decide to divert a large number of the new heavy bomb groups destined for the UK to a new strategic air force to be formed in the Mediterranean theatre of war. Officially activated on 1 November, the Fifteenth Air Force took over the heavy bombers of the Twelfth Air Force which were to be based in southern Italy. During the winter months the Fifteenth was built up to a complement of 21 heavy bomb groups, fifteen with B-24s and the remainder with B-17s. It was believed that better weather in the area would allow a greater rate of operations—although this was soon to prove otherwise, southern European winters being just as subject to poor weather as those further north. One major advantage of the Fifteenth Air Force's location was being in range of targets in eastern Europe that could not be reached from Britain, in particular the Romanian oilfields.

General Eaker protested at this diversion of forces for the Eighth Air Force. But Arnold had also decided that a change in command in England would be beneficial. With the cross-Channel invasion scheduled for spring 1944, the senior US air officer in the war with Germany, Lieutenant-General Carl Spaatz, was to return to the UK from North Africa and Eaker would be made the overall Allied air commander in the Mediterranean Theatre of Operations (MTO). This appeared to be a lack of faith in Eaker, who would have preferred to continue with the Eighth Air Force which he had worked so hard to secure. Arnold was an impatient man, answerable to a government investing colossal sums in a war-winning air force and one that wanted to see positive achievement.

Spaatz was to head a new overall organisation, eventually known as the United States Strategic Air Forces in Europe (USSTAF), a headquarters that was simply a redesignation of the Eighth Air Force HQ at Teddington; VIII Bomber Command HQ became the new Eighth Air Force. To carry out the strategic offensive, USSTAF had operational control over both the Eighth Air Force and the Mediterranean Allied Strategic Air Force (MASAF), comprising the US Fifteenth Air Force and No 205 Group RAF. For administration in matters such as bases, billets and rations MASAF came under the Supreme Allied Commander MTO, who had the authority to call upon Eaker should the land battle in Italy need the intervention of heavy bombers.

All this came into effect early in the New Year of 1944 as the Eighth Air Force's effective bomber strength reached nearly 800 'heavies'. The first major mission under the new leader (although the rest of the command staff remained much as before) came on 11 January when the weather prognosis held for clear skies over central Germany. The opportunity was seized to attack Pointblank targets, the aircraft industries. The two P-38 groups and the lone P-51 group were to give target cover. As it was prone to do, the weather deteriorated once the mission was launched, and most of the 2nd and 3rd Division forces heading for Brunswick received a recall. The remaining B-17s encountered strong opposition but were able to carry out a good attack on finding clear weather at the target. The 1st Division Fortresses sent to targets at Oschersleben and Halberstadt met the strongest enemy reaction to an Eighth Air Force mission since October and 42 failed to return. Against the total loss of 60 bombers the air gunners claimed 228 enemy aircraft shot down, a gross exaggeration even if claimed in good faith: the Luftwaffe's true losses in combat with the bombers appear to have numbered around 30 fighters. The mission illustrated yet again the dangers of deep penetrations, and but for the efforts of the sole Mustang group the 1st Division losses would have undoubtedly been greater.

Winter weather again restricted Eighth Air Force operations to 'blind' attacks with radar and, when possible, precision attacks on V-weapon sites and communication targets in occupied territories. Spaatz was prepared to bide his time for a high-pressure period, clear skies and more Mustangs. Major-General James H. Doolittle now commanded the Eighth Air

Below: The B-26 Marauders which were unfortunate in two low-level operations in May 1943 began flying at medium altitude—10,000 to 14,000ft—in July and had very low losses during the following three months. Flying in tight formations and usually escorted by RAF Spitfires, the aircraft had as their targets primarily enemy airfields, power supplies and communications in France and the Low Countries that lay within range. In mid-October the four groups of Marauders, with VIII Air Support Command to which they were assigned, were taken as the nucleus of the re-formed Ninth Air Force with a mission to support the forthcoming invasion of Normandy. Seen here sweeping over an Essex field (the light patches are where grain stooks stood), B-26B 118289/PN:W, *Colonel Rebel*, heads for home. Many of the Marauders that entered combat in the spring of 1943 were still in service two years later. (USAAF)

Above: Under full power, *Knock-Out Dropper* lifts away to the west from Molesworth's main runway. On 16 November, a few days after this photograph was taken, this Fortress, 124605/BN:R of the 359th Bomb Squadron, became the first in the Eighth Air Force to survive 50 combat missions. An original combat aircraft of the 303rd Bomb Group, it

had flown its first mission in November 1942 and went on to complete 75 before retirement to training use back in the USA. A J-type hangar, the corner of a T-2 and the control tower are visible in the background. (USAAF)

Below: An unprecedented five Medal of Honor awards, three posthumously, were made for the 1

August Ploesti operation. Col Leon Johnson received his decoration at a ceremony held on the 44th Bomb Group base, Shipdham, on 22 November 1943. On hand were Gen Devers, senior US Army commander in Europe at this time, and Gen Eaker. Here Johnson indicates the horizontal bomb symbol for participation in this low-level

mission on B-24D 123813/V of the 68th Bomb Squadron. Why someone thought the 44th's unofficial 'Flying Eightball' insignia should be hidden by a taped white sheet is not recorded. The aircraft's endurance was terminated on 21 January 1944 when shot down over France; it was the last of the group's original combat complement. (USAAF)

Force, having been brought from North Africa by Spaatz, whom he had served as commander of XII Bomber Command. An energetic man, Doolittle was best known for his leadership of the carrier-launched raid on Tokyo early in 1942.

Meanwhile RAF Bomber Command continued to raid Berlin, with four more major attacks during January, paying dearly for the destruction it added to this already well battered city. The 1,150-mile round trip took eight hours, with a constant threat of fighter interception in enemy airspace and over the North Sea, where the Luftwaffe had now extended its ranging. It was the lower-flying Halifaxes that took the brunt of the night fighter interceptions, losing 22 out of 264 on 20/21 and 26 out of 241 on 28/29 January. But the worst event for the Halifax squadrons was the abortive 21/22 January raid on Magdeburg when 35 never returned, a loss rate of 15.5 per cent. Feints and diversionary raids were a regular feature of the British raids in an effort to mislead the enemy raid controllers, sometimes successful but at times not. If it was still learning the countermeasures trade in some respects, No 100 Group played an increasingly important part in the deception plans. Yet there was no marked decline in attrition, and only the increasing strength of the bomber force reduced the percentage loss-to-sortie totals.

By February 1944 RAF Bomber Command was putting up more than a thousand aircraft on a night's operations, with

Above: While sunshine has found a gap in the November clouds, *Tar Heel Peggy* undergoes an engine test. The slipstream from Nos 3 and 4 whips the rain puddles from the Thurleigh hardstanding. The aircraft was one of the first B-17Gs received by the 306th Bomb Group, this model best distinguished by the so-called 'chin' turret under the nose. However, from a pilot's viewpoint the most important advance was the replacement of hydraulic turbo-supercharger controls by electric, thereby eliminating the high-altitude freezing difficulties that plagued the former. This particular B-17G, 239776 RD:K, was lost during Big Week operations with Lt John Coughlin's crew, half of whom were killed. (USAAF)

over 800 to a single target city to wreak havoc. Yet some of the small-scale raids often had more precise results, such as that carried out by No 5 Group's special duties squadron on 8/9 February against the Gnôme & Rhône aero-engine plant at Limoges. Success had mostly eluded this unit since its famous dam-busting raid. At Limoges the new CO, Wing Commander Leonard Cheshire, put into practice an idea for more assured accurate marking of a target by coming down to between 50 and 100ft and taking two runs over the target to make sure it was correctly identified. On his third low pass, target-markers were released directly over the factory buildings and these were then the aiming point for the eleven other Lancasters. The 12,000lb bombs dropped practically destroyed the factory. This was the first of several small-force raids carried out by the special duties unit against targets in France using techniques of this kind.

In the third week of February a high-pressure area settled over western Europe and Spaatz took the opportunity to launch Operation Argument, the most punishing series of attacks on the German aviation industry which became known to the Americans as Big Week. There had hitherto been little direct cooperation between the British and US bomber commands in a combined effort against specified targets, but on this occasion Harris committed RAF Bomber Command in strength. The series of attacks opened with a raid by 816 Lancasters and Halifaxes against Leipzig, with its many aviation related facilities, on the night of 19/20 February. Weather conditions being not as forecast caused the bomber stream to become somewhat disorganised, permitting the Luftwaffe its most successful night to date by depriving Bomber Command of 78 aircraft and crews. Once again it was the Halifaxes that suffered most cruelly, with 34 of the 255 despatched brought down, the majority of these being the underpowered Mk IIs and Vs. This outcome finally persuaded Bomber Command to withdraw these Merlin-engine models from long-range raids.

The following day the Eighth Air Force arrived over Leipzig, 417 1st Division B-17s bombing the depot airfield at Mockau and aviation factories in the area. Other aviation-related targets were sought by 2nd Division B-24s at Brunswick and Gotha and the 3rd Division B-17s at Tutow. In all, 1,003

Left, upper: As the distances between aircraft dispersal points and individual billets could be anything up to three miles on wartime airfields, a cycle was an essential means of transportation for the hard-worked 'erk'. Bicycles were in two categories—Service Pattern for standard Army models acquired by the RAF and Trade Pattern for those bought locally. When WAAFs came to need bicycles officially there was further classification as 'Bicycle, Male' and 'Bicycle, Female'! Mess time at Elvington brought scenes such as this on a bleak day in winter 1943. (IWM CH12529)
Left, lower: Halifax V LL126/ KN:W of No 77 Squadron at Elvington had a popular name derived from the W-William wireless call-letter. The hand-held .303-calibre machine gun was not rated very highly for defence and most bomb-aimers never had an opportunity to fire it in anger. (IWM CH12523)

Fortresses and Liberators were despatched that day, the American strength now equalling that of RAF Bomber Command in numbers.

Missing-in-action losses were relatively light—thirteen B-17s and eight B-24s—undoubtedly due to the effective fighter escort. Significantly, the US fighters claimed 61 of the enemy interceptors shot down, a figure that was near to the Luftwaffe's actual loss. Since its formation, most of the Fifteenth Air Force's missions had been of a tactical nature in support of ground forces in the MTO. Now Spaatz committed it to Argument, but heavy icing over the Alps led to an attempt to reach Regensburg on 20 February being called off.

In contrast to its misfortunes the previous night, RAF Bomber Command went to Stuttgart with a sizeable force, caused extensive damage to the Bosch electrical components factory and lost only nine bombers. On the 21st the Eighth Air Force struck at depot airfields in Germany and on the 22nd it went to Aschersleben and Schweinfurt. The opposition was fierce, as expected, and 41 bombers failed to return, but again the escort took a heavy toll of the enemy fighters, claiming 59. The Fifteenth Air Force was able to attack targets at Regensburg that day, the 183 B-17s and B-24s losing five. Weather held the Eighth down the next day, but the Fifteenth was able to send 120 B-24s to bomb a bearing factory at Steyr, Austria.

Right: What would the 'erk' have done without the leather jerkin? The ground crew is here conducting an engine test on *Oor Willie* on a cold winter's day. The Merlin XX was hard-met to give the Halifax a reasonable performance, even after eliminating the nose turret and introducing other weight-saving measures. LL126 was passed to the French squadrons formed at Elvington and later retired to No 1662 HCU. It was with this last unit that it met its end, diving into the ground near Long Ashton during a night navigation exercise. The seven members of the Polish crew were all killed. (IWM CH12526)

On 24 February the Eighth Air Force sent 809 bombers out to factories at Schweinfurt, Gotha and Rostock while the Fifteenth Air Force returned to Steyr. That night RAF Bomber command went to Schweinfurt with 734 bombers. On the morrow a strong force from the Eighth Air Force visited Regensburg, Augsburg, Stuttgart and Fürth. Regensburg was also attacked by the Fifteenth Air Force earlier in the day. Finally, before the weather deteriorated again, RAF Bomber Command went to Augsburg on 25/26 February, making an accurate attack which caused widespread damage.

The Big Week offensive against the German aviation and associated industries was judged by the post-war US Strategic Bombing Survey to have damaged 75 per cent of the plant buildings and structures which contributed to 90 per cent of aircraft production. At the time this destruction was believed to have produced a critical shortage of aircraft for the Luftwaffe. Their situation was certainly serious, but over the past year the dispersal of manufacturing had been speeded up and, with efficient repair organisations, recuperation was soon effected. What was more serious was the depletion of Luftwaffe fighter units that had contested the intrusions of the Eighth and Fifteenth Air Forces. For a total loss of 28 from 3,260 fighter sorties by British-based fighters and 413 from Italy, claims of over 200 enemy aircraft shot down were near to the true figure. The bomber gunners' claims ran far in excess of this total, and while the majority were unsubstantiated they had undoubtedly added to the attrition. The Luftwaffe could

make up the aircraft losses; finding experienced pilot replacements was another matter.

The bomber effort of Argument involved the despatch of some 3,300 sorties from the Eighth Air Force, 500 from the Fifteenth and 2,351 by the RAF. Loss totals were 137, 89 and 141 respectively, which was 6 per cent of the day force and 6.6 per cent for the night sorties.

As a prerequisite to the forthcoming invasion of Normandy, the Combined Chiefs of Staff had approved a plan to immobilise railway traffic within a 150-mile band behind the French coast. This was to be achieved by bombing marshalling yards, junctions and rail bottlenecks. Both Harris and Spaatz were against the involvement of the strategic air forces in this plan, believing that it should be left to the tactical bomber forces. But the scope of this project was far beyond the capabilities of the RAF Second Tactical Air Force and the US Ninth Air Force in the time available and the heavy bombers had to be involved. Despite his objections, Harris began to send small forces against selected French rail targets in late February and, with careful marking, obtained results with very light losses. Meanwhile it was the Americans who took up the onslaught on Berlin.

An attack on aviation industry targets in or near the enemy capital had been planned since November and was finally launched with some 750 bombers on 3 March. As so often happened, once the force was airborne and on its way, clouds gathered to hide the objectives, forcing targets of opportunity along the north-west coastline to be sought instead. The forecast was better for the next day, yet again the assault was frustrated by weather, extensive cloud and severe icing disrupting the formation of the bomber stream to such an extent that, once more, the majority of the force dropped on targets of opportunity in the Ruhr. One 3rd Division formation of 30 B-17s did carry on to Berlin and bomb the assigned target, to record a 'first' for the Eighth Air Force.

The conditions that the American bombers were seeking appeared on 6 March with little veiling cloud forecast for the Berlin area. A total of 730 B-17s and B-24s were despatched, and while clouds caused some formations to bomb targets of opportunity instead of the industries in Berlin suburbs, this mission evolved into one of the most vicious battles of the war for the Eighth Air Force and certainly its most costly. German raid controllers quickly identified the likely destination

of the bombers taking a more or less direct route to Berlin. When one of the combat wings was observed to have veered off course and to be lacking escort, Luftwaffe interceptors were directed to meet it and shot down twenty of the B-17s before Thunderbolts came to the rescue. Of the 30 bomb groups operating that day, 22 suffered losses, the total missing-in-action figure of 69 being the highest ever for an Eighth Air Force mission. Six other aircraft were written off through battle damage or accident and 347 of the returning Fortresses and Liberators sustained some form of battle damage. This epic mission saw the bomber gunners claim 97 enemy fighters destroyed, 28 probably destroyed and 60 damaged, the usual pattern of exaggeration stemming from a score of gunners all firing at the same fighter. More significant were VIII Fighter Command claims of 81 against the loss of eleven, for most of the 65 Luftwaffe aircraft known to have been lost this day went down to the American fighters. Half the US fighter claims were made by the three Mustang groups that were in action.

Two days later, the Eighth Air Force was at last able to put a significant proportion of more than a thousand tons of bombs carried to Berlin on the primary target, the bearing plants at Erkner. The losses were less severe, 37 bombers failing to re-

Left: A member of the ground crew signals to W Off H. Brunt as the latter brings Lancaster JB362/EA:D into its dispersal point at Fiskerton a few minutes before midnight after the Berlin raid of 22 November 1943. Four nights later this aircraft and Brunt's crew failed to return from another visit to Berlin. (IWM CH11642)
Below: Station personnel at Fiskerton look at the night flash photographs displayed at the techncal site following the 22/23 November Berlin raid. (IWM CH11647)

turn, as much of the enemy fighter opposition was intercepted by the escort. This time 79 Luftwaffe aircraft were claimed for the loss of eighteen Mustangs, Lightnings and Thunderbolts. The strain was beginning to tell on the Luftwaffe, for when 526 bombers were sent to Berlin the next day the enemy was conspicuous by his absence and the escort made no claims; bomber losses amounted to eight by flak and accident. A veil of cloud stretched beneath the bombers to frustrate their intentions, yet the lack of opposition was surprising.

Growing escort power was forcing the Luftwaffe fighters back to the borders of the Reich. The Germans' policy of concentrating their attacks on the US bombers and avoiding the escort had gradually put them at a disadvantage in that the experienced American fighter units were now seeking combat away from the bomber stream. Indeed, Generals Doolittle and Kepner (the latter of VIII Fighter Command) were now starting to use the long-range fighter as an offensive weapon. In January 1944 Kepner had given permission for fighters returning from escort duties to drop down and shoot up enemy airfields, a dangerous task but one that immediately began to have results. An extraordinary situation was developing: the Luftwaffe fighters were becoming the hunted not the hunters.

The Eighth Air Force did not return to Berlin until 22 March, when once again an undercast prevented strikes on aviation industry targets. Once more fighter opposition was noticeably absent, but it was not so for the RAF when Bomber Command resumed its offensive against this city on the night of 24/25 March. Harris sent 811 bombers, which found inclement weather and strong winds that dispersed the force and thereby the concentration of the bombing. In all, 72 Halifaxes and Lancaster failed to return. This proved to be the last major RAF Bomber Command raid on Berlin, and hereafter hitting the enemy capital was mostly left to the growing force of Mosquitos in No 8 Group's Light Night Striking Force, which amounted to eleven squadrons with more than 200 aircraft by the end of the war.

If the stinging losses from the Berlin raid were not bad enough, what occurred a week later on the last night of March was a disaster by the standards of operational assessment. Of 795 bombers sent to bomb Nuremburg, 64 Lancasters and 31 Halifaxes were lost. With a Halifax missing from a special operation over France, the total of 96 bombers was to be the highest loss of the war for a single night's operations. Undoubtedly the bright moonlight silhouetting the bombers against clouds contributed to the Luftwaffe's success, but what this staggering loss underlined was the fact that the night bomber was now more vulnerable than the day bomber in the western European sky. The darkness that originally hid the bomber from interception was now successfully penetrated by the night fighter's radar—and it was the night fighter that

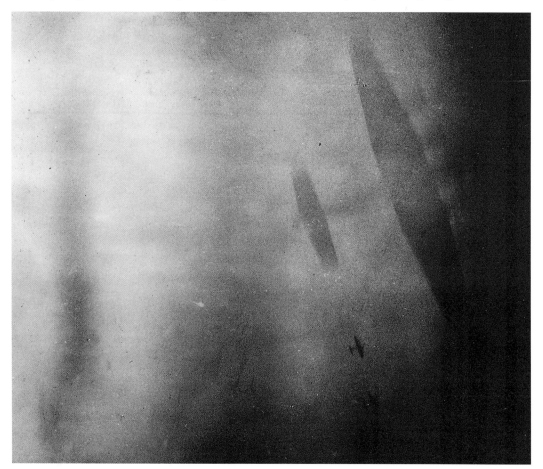

Left: The most damaging attack of the war on Berlin took place on 22/23 November 1943, carried out by the largest force sent up to that date, in total 764 Lancasters, Halifaxes, Stirlings and Mosquitos. The weather was poor, with extensive cloud over the enemy capital, and most of the 26 aircraft failing to return were thought to be victims of flak. As four Lancasters appear in this photograph of the attack, one suspects that some losses were caused by collision or descending bomb loads. (IWM C3920)

Right: Leipzig was cloud-covered on the night of 3/4 December 1943, when 527 Lancasters and Halifaxes were sent to this city in eastern Germany. Although cloud obscured the target area, the Pathfinder marking was very accurate and this proved to be the RAF's most damaging raid on Leipzig. Target-indicator flares show up well against the undercast in this photograph. (IWM C4033)

Right: A typical scene five miles high as an Eighth Air Force mission forges through the sub-stratosphere bound for an enemy target. The date is 13 December 1943 and the destination for the 1st Bomb Division is the shipbuilding facilities at Bremen. The higher formations are in the contrail band whereas the lower formations, in less cold and less humid air, escape these unwanted signs of their presence. A 'finger-four' flight of escort fighters weaves high above the bombers. (USAAF)

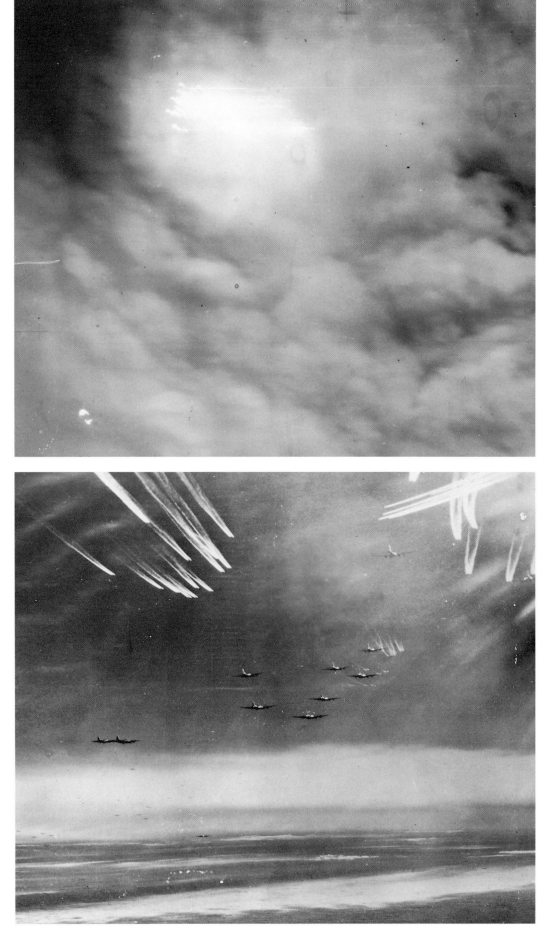

was protected by darkness, usually being able to stalk its victims unseen and having no bomber escorts to contend with.

Over the past few weeks No 100 Group had instigated regular Serrate patrols alongside the bomber streams with Mosquito night fighters. Occasional successes did little to minimise the Luftwaffe's operations against the bombers. Surprisingly, at this stage of the war the majority of RAF 'heavies' were still using the .303 calibre machine gun for defence despite its being outranged by cannon and heavy machine guns in enemy fighters. No 1 Group had been so annoyed by this situation that it had gone to a local manufacturer and installed a modified tail turret on its Lancasters with two .50 calibre weapons as used by the Americans in their bombers. This provided more positive defence through greater range and greater destructive power, but it was still no match for the heavy armament that the German twin-engine fighters carried. The advocates of the self-defending bomber in both Britain and America did nothing to give the bomber defensive armament equal to, or better than, that of the opposing interceptor.

On 1 April 1944 operational control of both the British and US strategic bomber forces passed to the Supreme Allied Commander for his direction in support of Overlord, the invasion of Normandy. The actual control directive was not issued until 14 April, but the Pointblank campaign had come to an end. The intermediate objective of neutralising the enemy air force was not complete but appeared to be happening. At this time it was adjudged primarily due to the destruction of aircraft manufacturing, whereas the principal attrition was through the continuing destruction of the Luftwaffe in the air by the long-range day fighters. The strategic bomber forces had yet to reach planned strength, and both Harris and Spaatz, in their different ways, still nurtured the belief that the bomber could be a war-winner. For the stoical bomber aircrews, who in the past sometimes had not much more than a fifty per cent chance of completing their tour of operations, better times were ahead—even though little more than a quarter of the bombs that would eventually be dropped on the Third Reich had so far been delivered.

Right, upper and lower: To give US bomber crews a close look at their antagonists, the RAF's No 1426 (Enemy Aircraft) Flight visted Eighth Air Force bases. Kimbolton was the venue for the FW 190A and Me 109F visit early in January 1944. The Focke-Wulf was captured after landing in error in the United Kingdom; the Messerschmitt, damaged by ground fire, put down near Beachy Head. (USAAF)

Below: By the beginning of 1944 the Lancaster was the dominant type in RAF Bomber Command, 36 of the 74 established squadrons being operational with the aircraft. To meet the engine demands of production, most new Lancasters leaving the factories were by this time fitted with the Packard version of the Merlin, built in the United States. Otherwise identical to Lancaster Is with British-built Merlins, those with the American engines were designated B Mk III. Here photographed above an undercast a few days after it was received by No 619 Squadron at Coningsby on 31 January 1944, Lancaster B.III LM446/PG:H would fail to return from an attack on the Gnôme-Rhône aero-engine factory at Gennevilliers, France, on 9/10 May 1944. It had 215 hours' flying time. (IWM CH21117)

Left: A train of sea mines arrives at a No 149 Squadron Stirling's dispersal at Lakenheath. A Stirling could accomodate six of these 1,500lb weapons, which descended by parachute after release. The mines, supplied by the Royal Navy, were either acoustic or magnetic, with many variations to elude enemy countermeasures. Stirlings laid 13,845 mines in 1942–44 and the task was not without its dangers: 84 Stirlings were missing and 26 were damaged by enemy action or crashed. For logistic planning, early in 1944 RAF vehicles were divided into classes. 'Type 2600' on this David Brown covered all classes of light tractors, so that for urgent

replacement, as necessary in the intense operations to come, the invasion of the continent, any other Type 2600 vehicle could be substituted. (IWM CH12674)
Top: Time for 'tiffin'. There was no let-up in the dropping of sea mines for Bomber Command, although this task was usually that of the Stirlings during the winter of 1943–44. Loading bomb bays was a tiring and tedious job, often conducted in unpleasant weather. Here No 149 Squadron armourers take a break for refreshment at bleak Lakenheath. (IWM CH12679)
Above: *Dante's Daughter* gets a '65th raid completed' symbol from ground crew member LAC E. Turner.

This Kirmington-based Lancaster of No 166 Squadron, officially ED731/AS:T2, started its operational service with No 103 Squadron in March 1943 and was passed to No 166 in September that year. It completed more than 70 sorties before being lost on 24/25 March 1944 in the last major RAF Bomber Command raid of the war on Berlin, when 72 'heavies' were lost. The 'scoreboard' acknowledges a DFC awarded to the pilot. The ice-cream symbols are for raids on Italian targets. (IWM CE126)

Above: The amused crowd gathered near a fire-water reservoir at Bassingbourn are present for the traditional dunking of an end-of-tour veteran. Major John C. Bishop, CO of the 323rd Bomb Squadron, enjoys the fun and comments on what immersion might do to his person . A veteran of many tough missions flown by the 91st Bomb Group, Bishop completed the 25th on a V-weapon site at La Glasserie, France, on 21 January 1944, which proved to be a 'milk run'. (USAAF)

Below: The trip to bomb the Luftwaffe airfield at Châteauroux/ Martinerie on 5 February 1944 looked like a 'milk run' to the men of the 401st Bomb Group compared with recent trips over Germany. In the event it proved to be anything but, some well-placed flak damaging eight aircraft, killing one gunner and wounding ten other airmen. Here, while other crew members look on helplessly, a seriously wounded airman is removed from their B-17, brought to a halt in the first empty parking space as soon as it had pulled off the runway at Deenethorpe. (USAF 65659AC)

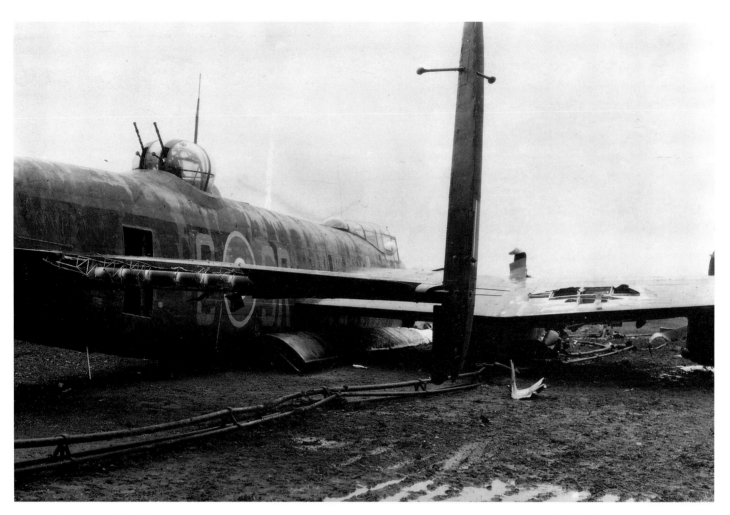

Above: A Lancaster of No 35 Squadron landing at Graveley, the first operational station to have FIDO (Fog Investigation and Dispersal Operation). Burning petrol and allied fuels, this apparatus successfully cleared fog from runways and was responsible for the safe landing of many bombers, particularly in the winter of 1944–45 when fifteen airfields were then equipped with FIDO. (IWM CH15271)

Below: No 101 Squadron started operations with Blenheims in No 2 Group; was transferred to No 3 Group and Wellingtons prior to converting to Stirlings; and when the Stirlings did not materialise transferred to No 1 Group, where it eventually received Lancasters. In October 1943 it was given a unique duty, the operation of Airborne Cigar (also known as ABC), making, in all, 2,477 sorties with this equipment. The aircraft carried special radios and a German-speaking operator, and Luftwaffe ground and airborne radio transmissions were sorted out and jammed. The No 101 Squadron aircraft so equipped were distinguishable by their large masts above the fuselage; these were usually eliminated by the censor in photographs that came his way, although he left one in this view of ME590/SR:C. The aircraft crash-landed at home base, Ludford Magna, on 26 February 1944, wrecking part of the FIDO pipework in the process. The squadron's aircraft normally carried a bomb load for the briefed target but were spread throughout the bomber stream. Flt Sgt R. Dixon took ME590 to Augsburg, where at 20,000ft his aircraft was hit by flak which fractured hydraulic lines. On the return flight he and his crew fell foul of an Me 110, whose fire perforated the elevators before the Lancaster could evade. ME590 was repaired, converted from Mk I to Mk III, and pensioned off to a Conversion Unit. (IWM CL3955)

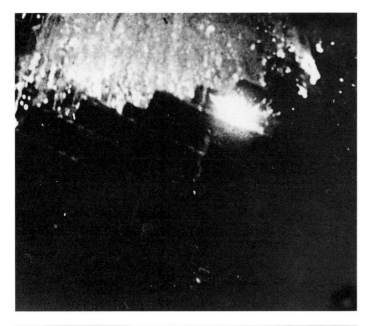

Far left: No 617 Squadron, the famous Dam-Busters, acquired a new CO early in 1944—the renowned G. L. Cheshire, now risen to a Wing Commander. Cheshire had been experimenting with low-level marking at night and was given permission to try this operationally against the Gnôme-Rhône aero-engine factory at Limoges. In bright moonlight on the night of 8/9 February 1944 he led twelve Lancasters, his, DV380/KC:X, armed with 140 ∞ 30 lb incendiaries and the others each with a 12,000lb bomb, to this target. Taking his Lancaster down to roof-top height, he made three runs over the factory to ensure correct identification and to warn French workers of the impending attack. There was little in the way of ground fire and on Cheshire's fourth pass the incendiaries were released. These three photographs show 30lb incendiaries exploding close to the factory building. (IWM C4086A)

Left: The Gnôme-Rhône plant under attack, with 12,000lb bombs bursting. Not only was production completely halted, but there were no reports of French casualties. None of the Lancasters was lost. So successful was this attack that No 617 Squadron was encouraged to pursue this technique on other small targets under cover of darkness. (IWM C4089)

Above: What eleven 12,000lb bombs did to the Gnôme-Rhône factory can be seen in the results of a photographic sortie next day. The machine shops housed in nine medium-sized and one large multi-bay building suffered severe damage. Out of 48 assembly bays, 21 were completely destroyed. The plant was built in 1939 as a main factory depot for the French Air Force. Under German management it was turned over to engine production for the Luftwaffe. (IWM C4166)

Above: In late February 1944 the first B-17s in natural metal finish began to arrive in the United Kingdom, it having been decided that camouflage paint was no longer necessary, being costly and having an adverse effect on performance. However, in combat operations there was a negligible difference in the performance of painted and unpainted aircraft. There was concern that the shiny metal would attract particular attention from enemy fighters and at first the 'silver' bombers were sent to selected groups who held back on their use until sufficient were on hand to enable a complete flight to be despatched on a mission. The 457th Bomb Group at Glatton was the recipient of some of the first metal-finish Fortresses, sending out the first, including this aircraft, on the 9 March 1944 mission to Berlin. Four days later the 457th flew the first 'all-silver' group formation—consisting of 21 B-17Gs—to be despatched by the Eighth Air Force. (USAAF)

Below left: No 106 Squadron Lancasters taxi out at Metheringham for Bomber Command's last major attack on Berlin, 24 March 1944. The runway lights are illuminated as one Lancaster starts its run. (IWM CH12560)

Above: The 392nd Bomb Group was more fortunate than most on the 6 March 1944 mission to Berlin in that only one of its number failed to return. B-24H 27598/E, *Flak Ducker*, was seen to have No 3 engine feathered before the target and to jettison its bombs. Lagging behind, it was last seen leaving the formation near the German border although still in normal flight. A wheels-down landing was attempted in a cow pasture at Overberg, the Netherlands, which was successful but for a collapsed nose wheel. Lt Erling Hestad and crew were all taken prisoner and the Luftwaffe presented with a little-harmed Liberator which they repaired and flew. (RNAF)

Above: Major Heinz Bär (behind the stooping Luftwaffe officer) was credited with 222 air victories between 1939 and 1945, of which some 20 were US heavy bombers. Here he examines a B-17 he brought down on 22 February 1944—the 323rd Bomb Squadron's 23040/OR:Q, *Miss Ouachita.* The stricken Fortress was crash-landed near Listrup. Two members of 2/Lt Spencer Osterberg's crew were killed in the action. (IWM GW208/1)

Left: The 392nd Bomb Group's 312 ∞ 500lb bombs impact on the dispersal area of St Dizier airfield, 24 March 1944. Preceding B-24 groups had hit the administrative area on the other side of the airfield. This was a fortuitous target of opportunity when the briefed target near Metz was found to be obscured by cloud. Airfields were favourite 'TOs' in occupied countries, being relatively easy to spot and large in area; moreover, an attack on such a target was less likely to result in local civilian casualties. (USAAF)

Above: The Skipper finishes his tour. Fg Off P. J. Ratham is 'chaired' by his crew on their return from the Frankfurt raid of 22/23 March 1944. (IWM CH12544)

Below: Airfield conditions in Italy were generally poor, with runways consisting of pierced steel plank or other metal reinforcement over soil or sod. Take-off accidents were far too common for the peace of mind of B-24 crews, particularly as the result was usually death or severe injury. Lt Peter Massare and crew were taking off at San Pancrazio in the 727th Bomb Squadron's B-24H 27765, *Little Butch*, on 29 March 1944

when the left tyre blew as the aircraft was close to lift-off. Efforts to maintain control were thwarted when the nose wheel collapsed. A dislodged No 2 propeller seriously injured the navigator but the rest of the crew got clear. There had been other 451st Bomb Group take-off crashes, but this was the first occasion that there had not been a fire and explosion. The Liberator was carrying ten 500lb bombs and 2,700 US gallons of fuel. (P. Massare)

Above left: Sqn Ldr P. Jousse DFC, of Rhodesia, a squadron navigation officer, goes over a point with an observer before the 30/31 March 1944 Nuremberg raid. (IWM CH12599)

Above: The station CO and other officers wait on the control tower at Snaith for the return of No 51 Squadron's Halifaxes from the disastrous raid of 30/31 March 1944. Five of the squadron's aircraft were missing and another crew were killed in a crash on return. (IWM CH12601)

Left: Italian airfields could spring some surprises: heavy rain turned Celone into a series of small lakes on one occasion. No 614 Squadron's Halifaxes shared the airfield with USAAF units. (IWM CNA 2685)

Right: Sometimes the strike camera, which was set in motion on the bomb run to record strikes, captured some unexpected moments. The 483rd Bomb Group was attacking the marshalling yard at Nis, Yugoslavia, from 21,000ft on 15 April when one of its B-17Fs, 25786 *Whizzer II*, took a direct flak hit between Nos 3 and 4 engines. The main fuel tanks took fire as the wing folded back, all in fractions of a second. All the crew members perished. 'There wasn't a hope in hell of getting out of that,' was the comment. (USAAF)

7
OVERLORD AND OIL

Although both Harris and Spaatz were now answerable to Eisenhower and Supreme Headquarters, Allied Expeditionary Forces (SHAFE) direction, for the time being operations continued along similar lines to those in the closing weeks of the Combined Bomber Offensive. RAF Bomber Command, with 83 squadrons, giving an average effective strength of over a thousand aircraft, pressed on with attacks on rail centres interspersed with the bombing of military targets in France and raids against German cities, mostly harbouring aviation-associated industries. In an effort to minimise French casualties, particular care was taken to mark targets accurately and Oboe-led pathfinder techniques were improved. Even so, some bombing would inevitably go astray. Churchill was among those who expressed concern about taking French lives and alienating the goodwill of that nation towards the Allied airmen. By and large these bombings were very accurate but there were French casualties, probably the worst occasion being at Lille on 9/10 April when a number of bombs fell on a housing area outside the rail yard target, killing some 450 persons.

The measures taken to identify and mark a target accurately cost the attacking force dear on occasion. Lancasters lingered too long in making a remarkably accurate attack on a fighting vehicle depot at Mailly-le-Camp on 3/4 May. Luftwaffe night fighters arrived and in the bright moonlight picked off 42 of the 338 bombers despatched. Generally, the losses during the

transportation and other operations over north-west France were light in comparison with trips into Germany. During this pre-invasion period most of RAF Bomber Command's activities over the Reich were in the Ruhr area, where pathfinders produced their most accurate target marking. It was the Eighth Air Force that continued to push deep into the enemy homeland, still pursuing the destruction of aviation industries and deliberately challenging the Luftwaffe to a fight.

On 11 April Oschersleben and Sorau were the main objectives for 917 Fortresses and Liberators. Several air battles developed and the total of 64 bombers lost ran near to the record

Right: The accuracy of Oboe marking on short-range targets was often amazing. As part of the campaign to deny the Wehrmacht the use of the railways in northern France, Juvisy-sur-Orge was one of the targets on 18/19 April 1944. No 5 Group sent 202 Lancasters with four supporting Mosquitos to bomb on the Pathfinder marking of three No 8 Group Oboe Mosquitos. No trains would run here for some time, as this photograph, taken the following afternoon, clearly shows. Warehouses, repair shops, signalling apparatus and most other facilities were completely demolished. (IWM C4297)

Far right: Fg Off C. Rodgers and crew of No 630 Squadron's Lancaster ME739/LE:D after landing at 0126hrs on 19 April 1944. The Juvisy raid was the first operational sortie for the aircraft. It would serve the squadron well for twelve months, being lost on the Leipzig operation of 10/11 April 1945, exactly a year after its delivery to East Kirkby. (IWM CH12777)

loss of the 6 March Berlin mission. For some months the Luftwaffe had been employing special interception units known as *Sturmgruppen* (storm groups) which employed heavily armed and armoured FW190s in mass attacks to saturate the defensive fire of the bomber formations. This proved to be the most effective means of attacking the B-17 and B-24 formations, and *Sturmgruppen* continued to make occasional and successful interceptions over the months ahead. Their drawback was the unwieldy nature of the heavily weighted FW190s which made them relatively easy prey to US escort fighters, as on this day when several were accounted for in the total of 73 of the enemy shot down. All but three of these claims were registered by Mustang pilots; six groups were now flying the type. But it was not only in the air that the Luftwaffe suffered attrition. The American fighters picked off 132 enemy aircraft on their airfields before returning to England, an assessment of gun camera film rating 65 as destroyed.

The grinding down of the Luftwaffe fighter arm continued throughout April and May as Spaatz sent his bombers far and wide. The Fifteenth Air Force in Italy, hitherto putting most of its effort into attacking communication targets in its theatre of operations, was afforded sufficient escort to allow more ventures into Austria and southern Germany, attacking Wiener Neustadt industry on 23 April. But it was the Eighth that con-

tinued to force the pace. When 754 bombers went to targets in south-west Germany on 24 April the escort again had a field day, with claims of 70 in the air and 57 on the ground. Even so, 40 of the 'heavies' failed to return. Five days later Berlin was the bait and cost 63 of the 679 bombers despatched, mainly to *Sturmgruppe* activity when the escort was absent; the US fighters could only catch sixteen of the enemy. Berlin was again the objective on 7 May but the Luftwaffe stayed away, relying on the 'solid undercast' to protect important installations from American bombs. The next day was a different matter, when better weather provoked the German fighters to challenge some 800 bombers heading for the Berlin and Brunswick areas. The 'heavies' lost 36, the escort thirteen, with claims of 55 against the Luftwaffe. The offensive tended to be seen as a numbers business by many observers, but these statistics showed that the enemy had lost air superiority in his airspace. That single-seat fighters would fly up to 500 miles from their bases and command the sky was thought neither possible nor realistic four years earlier; yet it had become fact. The Luftwaffe could and would challenge the American missions as opportunity and forces allowed, but it was in decline.

Spaatz had long seen oil and the petroleum industry as the enemy's Achilles' heel. The Romanian oilfields were still a major source of natural oil. Germany, aware that oil importa-

Above: One of the most distinguished squadrons in RAF Bomber Command was No 460, an RAAF unit. Being a three-flight squadron with an establishment of 30 aircraft for virtually the whole time it was equipped with Lancasters, it claimed to have hauled more bombs into the Reich than any other squadron in the Command. It did this at great cost, suffering heavy losses on many occasions. One Lancaster that escaped the attrition was W4783/AR:G from its original complement received in 1942, which endured through 90 raids. After completion of the 90th trip on 20/21 April 1944 the authorities decided to retire the veteran and present it to the Australian War Museum. Posing for the camera is Fg Off J. A. Critchley's crew, who flew the aircraft on its final trip. Although No 460 was an Australian squadron, many air crew members were British—in this crew the flight engineer and the two air gunners. A Binbrook C-type hangar can be seen in the background of this photograph. (IWM CH20519)

tion by sea would be denied in wartime, had long been developing and increasing a synthetic-oil industry, and British Air Ministry strategists, recognising this, had listed oil as the top priority in Bomber Command's early directives. That this priority had been dropped was because mounting the precision attacks necessary had not been possible in the early years of the war. Spaatz, having the power to begin such a campaign (although official sanction was not bestowed at this juncture), could be justified in assaulting oil targets as a means of bringing the Luftwaffe to battle. Under this pretext Doolittle sent 886 bombers to Merseburg, Lützendorf, Zwickau, Brux, Zeitz and Bohlen on 12 May. It is likely that the objectives were recognised by the German raid controller, for the Luftwaffe committed its fighters in strength and suffered severely at the hands of the American fighters, which claimed 71. The bombers wrought significant destruction on most targets, at a cost of 46 of their number. Six days later Spaatz launched the Fifteenth Air Force in the first of a series of direct attacks against the Ploesti refineries, with 206 bombers over the target. Since

early April the Fifteenth had carried out five missions against the rail facilities at Ploesti as part of its brief to destroy transportation. As elsewhere, the Germans put up a strong defence of their oil supplies and this mission cost fourteen bombers.

The Eighth Air Force successfully provoked the Luftwaffe on 19 May with another mission to Berlin that cost the enemy 70 fighters if the claims were true. The enemy capital was again visited on 24 May, and over a thousand B-17s and B-

24s went to oil targets on 28 and 29 May to round off its intrusions into Germany before the launch of Overlord. Throughout April and May the Eighth Air Force had also honoured its commitment to SHAFE requirements with attacks on communications and airfield targets in France and the Low Countries. In April 72 per cent of its effort had been against such targets and in May 55 per cent. RAF Bomber Command put 70 per cent of its effort to the invasion plan targets in April and 82 per cent in May. Then, for a few weeks, both forces concentrated nearly all their effort on Overlord, bombing coastal defences and fortifications from the Scheldt to Brest with one bomb in the invasion area for two elsewhere in order not to identify the real area of intent.

A total of 1,136 RAF Bomber Command 'heavies' dropped 5,315 tons of high-explosive bombs in the pre-landing attack on Normandy defences and the Eighth Air Force 'heavies' followed up with two missions when 1,622 aircraft dropped 4,852 US tons. The RAF 2nd Tactical Air Force and the US Ninth Air Force bombers added further to these totals.

On the morning of D-Day the last of the assigned US heavy bomber units become operational, an Eighth Air Force Liberator group. Spaatz then had 62 heavy groups, 41 in Britain and 21 in Italy, with approximately 2,500 and 1,250 aircraft respectively. B-17s equipped 27 groups and B-24s 34; one group, a pathfinder organisation, had a mixed force. Because of the difficulty of operating B-17s and B-24s in the same task force, the Eighth Air Force's 3rd Division converted the five B-24 groups it had received to B-17s, the preferred type, during the summer and autumn of 1944. The complement of a US heavy bomber squadron had been almost doubled since the Eighth Air Force arrived in Britain, from nine to sixteen aircraft. That of an RAF Bomber Command squadron had also advanced, to twenty and, where a third flight had been formed, to thirty. However, while the US strategic air forces had reached full strength, RAF Bomber Command would expand further.

During the days following the Allied landings the heavy bombers hauled a prodigious quantity of ordnance to continental Europe, mostly to meet the tactical needs of the ground forces. The inclement weather often prevented the Eighth Air Force, with its high-altitude precision method, from attacking, whereas RAF Bomber Command would often employ low-altitude marking, with the bombers coming down to between 2,000 and 6,000ft below the clouds at attack. In consequence, whereas only 30 per cent of the Eighth Air Force effort was against targets to meet invasion requirements, some 80 per cent of the British 'heavies'' business was of a tactical nature. In fact, RAF Bomber Command carried out no major raids on targets in Germany during June 1944 and then, despite his declared opposition to what he called 'panacea target

Below: B-24 groups arriving in England and Italy during the winter of 1943–44 were equipped with the B-24H and J models. These featured improved armament, with a power-operated nose turret and a retractable ball turret. Unfortunately these features and revised equipment raised the overall weight of the Liberator, adversely effecting handling qualities as well as reducing operational altitude when fully loaded. The 701st Bomb Squadron's B-24J 2100404/ MK:S, *The Grim Reaper*, endured to the end of hostilities despite its forbidding name, although it was transferred to another group following repairs. The ball turret usually remained retracted until over enemy territory due to its drag when lowered; the guns can be seen pointing down from the well. To improve handling, most Eighth Air Force Liberators had their ball turrets removed in the spring of 1944, but the Fifteenth Air Force chose to retain theirs. (USAAF)

systems', Harris added his weight to the gathering assault on the enemy oil industry by hitting storage and synthetic plants in the Ruhr.

On 14 June RAF Bomber Command carried out its first major daylight raid by heavy bombers since October 1942, albeit an evening attack using pathfinder markers. A force of 221 Lancasters with thirteen Pathfinder Mosquitos was sent to Le Havre, where light German naval craft were active against the invasion fleet. The next day an even stronger force carried out a similar bombing of Boulogne for the same purpose. Although apparently successful in surprising the naval activity, both attacks cost many French lives. Only one bomber was lost from each of these daylight raids, which were supported by strong fighter escort—all in sharp contrast to what happened on the night of 24/25 June when Luftwaffe night fighters were responsible for most of 22 bombers lost attacking seven flying-bomb sites near the French coast. The message that night had become more dangerous than day for the British 'heavies' was emphasised on several occasions during the weeks following, not more so than on 7 July when flak claimed the only loss from 467 aircraft putting down 2,350 tons of HE in 38 minutes on troop positions near Caen. That night 221 Lancasters and Mosquitos seeking V-weapon storage sites lost 31 of their number. German night fighters could still operate in the sky almost with impunity, whereas the day fighters could only manage the occasional hit-and-run in the invasion area. Allied air superiority was supreme in daylight. Once on the ground it was a completely different situation for the Luftwaffe night fighters. A growing effort by intruder aircraft of No 100 Group against the airfields from which they operated and frequent strafing attacks by Allied day fighters were disabling or destroying an increasing number of these Me 110s and Ju 88s. Throughout the summer of 1944 RAF Bomber Command had some operations against the enemy in every 24-hour period and nearly half of these were carried out in daylight.

If weather often prevented the Eighth Air Force from bombing in occupied France, Spaatz and Doolittle took full advantage of fair weather over Germany. The oil industry was now the predominant objective, with four major mission days in June, three in July and four in August, but with clearer skies on many days in the later months more weight was directed against communication targets to prevent reinforcements and supplies reaching the battle front. The forces available to Spaatz had become so great that it was common for a day's operations to take in up to a score of different briefed targets. The Fifteenth Air Force, with no pressing demands from the Italian ground campaign, continued its onslaught on Ploesti. In fourteen missions an average of 300 bombers caused such destruction to the refinery plant that output was reduced to one-fifth of normal production. The Fifteenth found, as the

Eighth had, that the enemy defended his oil supplies at all cost. The flak defences at Ploesti were some of the strongest in Europe and were responsible for most of the 174 bombers lost on these missions.

Placing part of the strategic bomber force in southern Italy continued to be somewhat of a disappointment during the winter months as the Italian weather proved as severe and fickle as that encountered in northern Europe. Additionally there was the considerable obstacle of the Alps to avoid or fly over, making forays into southern Germany extremely difficult in inclement conditions. With the coming of spring and summer the southern European weather was much more given to clear skies than further north, and the Fifteenth Air Force was able to carry out some excellent attacks. The RAF had a small number of Wellington and Halifax squadrons for night operations with No 205 Group in Italy. With the joint command system of the MTO, these operated under Fifteenth Air Force target policy and in some cases shared the same bases as the Americans.

To enable targets in the easternmost part of the Nazi empire to be brought within range of the B-17s and B-24s, arrangements were made with the Soviets for the use of specified airfields in the Ukraine. It was planned that bombers would leave their British or Italian bases and after bombing fly on to land in the USSR. There they would be refuelled and re-armed for attacking another target on the way back to home bases. The first of these shuttle missions was flown by 170 B-17s of the Fifteenth Air Force with a P-51 escort on 2 June, bombing a Hungarian marshalling yard. The return flight on 6 June took in a Romanian target. On 21 June it was the Eighth Air Force's turn when 145 of the 3rd Division Fortresses from the 1,111 bombers out that day bombed a target near Berlin and flew on to land in Russia. Unfortunately, the formation was shadowed by a Luftwaffe reconnaissance aircraft and that night a strong force of German bombers attacked the Fortresses' Poltava base. Meeting no effective defences, the enemy had considerable success, destroying 44 B-17s and damaging 26. The surviving Fortresses flew on to Italy a few days later, bombing a target en route, and from Italy back to the United Kingdom.

The main weight of the USAAF heavy bomber attacks continued to be against oil whenever attacks on tactical targets in support of the ground forces were not required. There were attacks against 26 separate oil industry targets in June, sixteen in July and 44 in August. The RAF contributed ten, seventeen and six target raids respectively during these months. The effect was to cut the overall production of petroleum-related products by about half at the end of these three months and create serious shortages in many branches of the Wehrmacht.

The Germans, appreciating the vulnerability of their synthetic oil industries, had taken countermeasures, including

Right: Back from bombing Nancy/Essay airfield, a Luftwaffe fighter base, crew members relax in the interrogation room at Deenethorpe, 27 April 1944. A cigarette and whisky helped, each crew member being entitled to a measure of the latter if he wished; those who didn't passed theirs to those who did—lucky the drinker who had a teetotal crew! Oranges, rare in wartime England, were also available at Deenethorpe, it appears. (USAF 65568AC)

Right: Stiff opposition was met on the 29 April 1944 mission to Berlin, with 63 of the Eighth Air Force 'heavies' missing. The 613th Bomb Squadron's 231116/IW:O, *Cawn't Miss*, was shot down by fighters and crashed in the formal garden of a house at Liers, Belgium. Pilot 2/Lt J. H. Singleton and four of his crew escaped and evaded capture. The other members of the crew were killed in the action. A member of the Belgian household secretly took this photograph of German soldiers surveying the wreck. (F. F. Kaye)

Right: The attack on the Panzer depot at Mailly-le-Camp on 3/4 May 1944 was outstandingly successful in the destruction caused, which included more than a hundred vehicles, many of them tanks. For a French target it brought some of the most grievous losses ever suffered by Bomber Command heavies—42 of the 346 Lancasters sent. Delay, occasioned by faulty radio tuning and other factors, allowed the Luftwaffe night fighter force to arrive on the scene, with dire consequences. The Lancaster caught in this photograph appears to have lost its port inner engine. (IWM C4335)

Left, upper: P Off R. R. Reed of No 576 Squadron did a remarkable job of piloting and was awarded a well-deserved DSO for bringing back ME703/UL:S2 from the costly raid on Mailly-le-Camp. Enemy fire shattered the rear turret, killing the gunner. Elevators and rudders were damaged, as were the oxygen and electrical systems. Because of the electrical failures the radiator flaps were inoperative, causing engine overheating. The rear turret wreckage made control so difficult that Reed had to have help from both the flight engineer and bomb-aimer in order to keep pressure on the control column and rudder pedals. (IWM CE148)
Left, lower: Wellington MF139:K of No 37 Squadron, with spring flowers around Ju 88 wreckage left

by the former occupants of Tortorella. The trusty 'Wimpy' still soldiered on with night bombing operations in the Mediterranean area, this one failing to return from Brod Bosanski on 15 July 1944. (IWM CNA4207/1)
Above: Acrid smoke rises from the oil farm at Campina, 20 miles north-west of Ploesti, as a result of a night visit by RAF Halifaxes and Wellingtons from Italy in the early hours of 6 May 1944—one of the first stabs at the Ploesti area oil production facilties, which were supplying between 30 and 40 per cent of Germany's needs at this time. The photograph was taken by an SAAF Mosquito the following day. (IWM C4346)

An estimated 400 Luftwaffe fighters took to the air, to be met by a similar number of Mustangs, which by then equipped ten of the fifteen Eighth Air Force fighter groups. The German fighters were responsible for bringing down the majority of the 39 'heavies' lost, but the American fighters claimed their biggest score yet, 115 against seventeen of their own number. Even allowing for incorrect assessment of gun camera film in some cases, this outcome was growing evidence of the crisis in competent pilots within the German fighter units. On occasions the US pilots had been able to shoot down as many as four or five of the enemy during a single sortie, their victims appearing to have little experience in air fighting. On the two following days the Luftwaffe again rose in strength to combat the Eighth Air Force and again suffered heavily.

While often lacking replacement pilots, the Luftwaffe never experienced a serious shortage of fighter aircraft. Despite the punishing assaults of Big Week and the prolonged campaign against the German aviation industries in the spring, aircraft production had actually risen and would reach nearly 40,000 units by the end of the year, whereas total production for 1943 was only just over 25,000. This was in part due to dispersal of manufacturing and in part to speedy repair of the bombed installations through the brilliant organisation of Albert Speer, Hitler's overlord of war production.

dummy sites, camouflage, smokescreen apparatus and protective blast walls. Additionally, considerable flak defences had been placed in the area of the plants and were reinforced. It was in defence of oil that the Luftwaffe would occasionally offer spirited challenge to the American bombers. This occurred on 11 September when 1,131 'heavies' set off for Ruhland, Misburg and Merseburg, with part of the force briefed to make the third shuttle to the USSR from British bases.

Above: Project Grapefruit was the evaluation of a device designed to allow bombers to avoid passing through the anti-aircraft artillery of a heavily defended target. Wings and empennages were strapped to a standard M-34 2,000lb bomb and these 12ft-span glide bombs were suspended, one each from wing shackles on a B-17. The 41st Combat Wing was given the task of employing this weapon, in which, incidentally, the Eighth Air Force had little faith. After much experimentation the first and last glide bomb mission was run against Cologne/Eifeltor marshalling yard on 28 May 1944. The release was made some miles from Cologne but unexpected winds at altitude distributed the missiles far and wide, with no worthwhile damage in the target area. Two of these glide bombs are seen suspended under a 303rd Bomb Group B-17 at Molesworth. (USAF. A61924AC)

Left: Probably the most telling photograph of the Fifteenth Air Force campaign against the Ploesti oilfields is this action shot of Liberators passing through an intense flak barrage against a backdrop of blazing oil storage tanks on 31 May 1944. Sixteen of the 481 attacking aircraft were lost this day. (USAAF)

Right: The first 'shuttle' mission to the USSR was flown on 2 June 1944 by the Fifteenth Air Force with 130 B-17s and a Mustang escort. The target was the marshalling yards at Debrecen, and, after bombing, the Fortresses continued on to land at Poltava and Mirgorod in the Ukraine. Russian officers were present at Poltava as the 97th Bomb Group's contingent landed. The B-17G about to touch down is 2102918, *Idiot's Delight*, of the 342nd Bomb Squadron. It fell to flak at Munich on 19 July 1944. (USAAF)

Below: Communications targets preoccupied the strategic bombers from England following the Normandy invasion. This section of 446th Bomb Group Liberators are releasing 500-pounders on the smoke-marker drop (right) of the leader for a strike on a rail bridge near Tours, 15 June 1944. The curling smoke trail is from the preceding section. The target was claimed to have been demolished. (USAAF)

Meanwhile RAF Bomber Command, having paid particular attention to German oil storage sites in France during July and August, ventured across the German border on 27 August with 216 Halifaxes plus a pathfinder force and Spitfire escort to bomb the Homberg/Meerbeck synthetic plant on Oboe marking. This was the first major raid by the Command on a German target in daylight since August 1941. Other daylight raids on a similar scale were soon to become commonplace and continue almost to equal night operations in number. Harris had also returned his bombers to city attacks in late July, but these were not on the scale seen during the previous winter. These renewed area attacks were to be of some concern in British quarters, for while Darmstadt was a rail centre its devastation on 11/12 September and some 12,000 casualties seemed an unnecessarily heavy blow. But, as this was at the time of the V-weapon bombardment of London and southeast England, there was little charity towards the German nation.

On 14 September 1944 the strategic air forces were released from their direction by the Supreme Allied Commander. At this date it might be thought that the strategic bombing effort was drawing to a close. In fact, of the total tonnage dropped on Germany during the Second World War, near two-thirds had yet to be delivered.

Left: A B-24 of the 460th Bomb Group falls victim to an Me 109's attack near Vienna during the Fifteenth Air Force's strike against synthetic oil plants in the area on 16 June 1944. The crew were able to bale out before the aircraft went out of control and broke in two. The B-24 in the foreground, 41-28804, is an all-over grey-painted pathfinder with ground-scanning H2X radar. (IWM EA29146)

Below: The success of oil target attacks was often very evident through the columns of black smoke that rose many thousands of feet. This is one of five oil farms struck at Hamburg on 20 June 1944. The strike of the 303rd Bomb Group has been recorded by the camera in B-17G 297058/BN:V, *Scorchy II*, at 0924hrs from 26,000ft. The target of another formation burns in the bottom right-hand corner of the photograph. (USAAF)

Right, top: Burnt-out carcasses of 96th Bomb Group B-17s at Poltava, where Luftwaffe night bombers put half the force out of action, 47 being adjudged destroyed and 24 damaged. Soviet airfield defences were known to be weak, but this attack was unexpected. It was probably the most successful outcome of any Luftwaffe attack on an Allied airfield. (W. G. Gaither)

Right, centre: During a daylight bombing of enemy forces at Villers-Bocage on 30 June 1944, No 75 Squadron Lancaster ND917 was hit by flak splinters, one striking flight engineer Sgt P. McDevitt in the knee and causing excessive bleeding. The pilot, Sqn Ldr N. Williamson, seeing that McDevitt was losing blood rapidly, elected to land on one of the Advanced Landing Grounds on the Normandy beach-head, where medical attention could be sought. This was the first RAF 'heavy' to make use of one of these small strips. The photograph, taken next day, shows Williamson presenting bomb-aimer Fg Off G. Couth with Camembert cheese produced in the district to mark his 23rd birthday. Other members of the crew are Fg Off J. Watts, navigator; Sgt J. Russell, rear gunner; Sgt R. Jones, mid-upper gunner; and Sgt S.Cooke, wireless operator. ND917 was one of four Lancasters lost during a daylight raid on Solingen on 4 November 1944. (IWM CL291)

Right, bottom: The vital rail bridge at Theoule-sur-Mer, France, was the target for 56 Liberators from Italy on 12 July 1944 and they were successful in their objective of blocking a supply route to the German naval base at Toulon. Here two 450th Bomb Group B-24s turn away in perfect visibility, with the smoke and dust caused by their bombs veiling the target. (USAF. 61992AC)

Left, top: More punishment for Ploesti. A cameraman took this picture of the 45lst Bomb Group's *Screamin' Meemie II* at 23,000ft against a backdrop of burning oil clouds. This mission involved an attack by 607 bombers which dropped 1,526 US tons—the largest weight on Ploesti oil in any mission. Twenty bombers failed to return. (USAAF)

Left, centre: When the ground crew of Halifax LW473/LK:Q at Burn came to inspect the bomber prior to an operation on 27 May 1944 they discovered that a swarm of bees had taken up residence in an aperture in the port rudder. The flight sergeant in charge sent for Mr Webster, an apiarist who lived in a village adjoining the airfield. While aircrew look on, the apiarist uses his skills to remove the intruders so that No 578 Squadron's Q-Queen can go to war. (IWM CH13294)

Left, bottom: Production of the Hercules-powered Lancaster II was limited to 300 machines, all built by Armstrong-Whitworth. Although faster than the Mk I and III, the radial-engine model did not provide such a good ceiling. However, the air-cooled engines were considered more dependable, with less servicing attention required. No 514 was the last squadron to use the mark operationally. Captained by Fg Off C. B. Sandland, Lancaster Mk II LL734/JI:O is seen here flying its 33rd sortie during the 27 July attack on the V1 site at Les Catelliers, one of a dozen No 514 aircraft that each dropped eighteen 500-pounders on Oboe marking. (IWM C561)

Right, upper: To hamper German naval activities in the Mediterranean in preparation for the Allied landings in southern France, the Fifteenth Air Force was sent against the Toulon docks on 6 August 1944. The flak defences were moderate but accurate, and a strike camera covering the 376th Bomb Group's drop also picked up a Liberator with a considerable length of the right wing's trailing edge shot away. The damage did not stop the bomber returning safely to base, however. (USAF 61990AC)

Right, lower: Members of Lt Bernard Ball's crew remove their flying clothes while shaded from the August sun as other men of the 449th Bomb Group survey the damage to their Liberator. A direct hit by an 88mm shell blasted away the top of the fuselage and killed the two waist gunners during an attack on a communications target in Yugoslavia. Ignoring the risk that the aircraft might break in two, and having lost most tail surface control, Ball brought the aircraft back to Bari using changes in engine power to manoeuvre and make a safe landing. This photograph also illustrates that the main force of a flak shell explosion was upwards. (USAAF)

Left, top: Battle damage, bad weather or diminishing fuel often brought British bombers to American bases and vice versa. These Halifaxes and a Lancaster found refuge at Attlebridge, where they were parked on an out-of-service runway which was being 'patched'. One of the Halifaxes is from No 102 Squadron at Pocklington and five from No 346, a Free French-manned squadron stationed at Elvington. All had been engaged in daylight attacks on enemy airfields on 3 September 1944, the fifth anniversary of the outbreak of war, (S. Clay)

Left, centre: The long-range fighter that is generally considered to have saved the day for the USAAF daylight bombing campaign. With a performance superior or on a par with that of its two principal Luftwaffe opponents, the Mustang could range anywhere the bombers were likely to go. This is a flight of P-51Ds of the 357th Fighter Group, one of the most successful Mustang units in air combat. (USAAF)

Left, bottom: The US day bombers made increasing use of radar devices to locate and attack targets as the war progressed. H2X, the US-built and improved version of the RAF's H2S ground-scanning radar, was synchronised with the Norden bomb sight computations to obtain more accurate 'blind' drops. Each bomb group built up its own pathfinder teams as more PFF aircraft became available. Cloud hindered visual attack on 14 August 1944 when the Eighth Air Force sent over 1,000 bombers to strike airfields in Germany and France. The 401st Bomb Group lead, 297947/ SC:U, has the radar scanner lowered from the aperture that held the ball turret on standard B-17s. The bombardier is making a visual run on Hagenau with radar back-up if cloud foils his aim at the last moment. In the distance are the wind-whipped smoke markers from a previous formation, fading flak bursts and other bombers. (USAAF)

Right: The most infamous of targets for the Eighth Air Force was Merseburg, which had the most concentrated flak defences in the Reich to defend the precious synthetic oil plants of the area. Repeated attacks were necessary to check production as after each bombing feverish repair activity took place using a mass of foreign labour quartered in the neighbourhood. This unusual view of a Merseburg bomb run on 11 September 1944 was taken from the ball turret of a 381st Bomb Group Fortress at 27,500ft. The flak is yet to come. Of 1,016 bombers attacking oil targets that day, 39 were missing and another eight write-offs through damage. (USAAF)

Below: When the Russians captured the Ploesti area they were considerably impressed by what the USAAF and RAF had done, if not very willing to let their allies access the results themselves. The Concordia Vega Refinery was a major target on several occasions and the devastation is plain to see in this low-level photograph taken by a US reconnaissance aircraft on 24 September 1944. (USAAF)

8
THE MAJOR ASSAULT

The USAAF strategic bomber forces had reached planned strength during the summer of 1944 but the numbers of aircraft actually diminished during the winter of 1944–45 when a start was made on transferring units to re-train on the B-29 Superfortress for operations against Japan. RAF Bomber Command, however, was still expanding, with the formation of a score more squadrons during the autumn and early winter of 1944. The total passed the hundred mark in October and had reached its summit, 108, early in the New Year. This gave the Command a strike force of some 1,500 bombers—still half the total of the combined US bomber organisations, but the British 'heavies' had twice the bomb load capability of the B-17s and B-24s over the same ranges. Lancasters, prime heavy bombers in RAF Bomber Command, had replaced the last Stirlings in No 3 Group the previous September. They had also become the standard 'heavies' in No 8

Pathfinder Group and, with production of the type in Canada, were being used to re-equip squadrons in No 6 (Canadian) Group. In Yorkshire, No 4 Group remained an all-Halifax formation, the late production of this design having greater power and reliability than earlier models.

Most noticeable in RAF Bomber Command's operations during the later half of 1944 had been the improvement in bombing accuracy. A combination of factors was responsible, chiefly improved target-marking techniques, the most successful being made at very low altitudes. The improvement in radar devices and their operation was another reason for fewer instances of widely scattered bombs. More reliable H2S ground-scanning radar and the training of operators were other factors. Oboe still gave the most accurate target location and continued to be used for most night attacks within its range. Another radar-ranging device, known as G-H and introduced

Left: It was estimated that by the autumn of 1944 a quarter of Eighth Air Force bombers would sustain some flak damage and that for every thirteen aircraft damaged one would be lost. The 508th Bomb Squadron's 298004/YB:H never flew again after the 27 September 1944 mission, although it was not counted as a loss. Over Cologne an 88mm shell entered the fuselage near the radio room rear entrance, the explosion blasting away the ball turret and killing the gunner, Sgt Kenneth Divil. There was a special radio operator on board at this location, Sgt John Kurtz, a German-speaker who was monitoring enemy transmissions for the Y Service. He fell from the aircraft and survived as a POW. Capt G. Geiger, seen surveying the damage, kept control and made a safe landing. (USAAF)

Right: Flying from a temporary Russian base, 28 Lancasters of Nos 9 and 617 Squadrons attacked the battleship *Tirpitz* (indicated by the arrow) in Kaa Fjord, north Norway, on 15 September 1944. The smokescreen did not stop some accurate bombing and the vessel was hit by one of the thirteen Tallboys dropped. This and other damage rendered *Tirpitz* unserviceable for sea action and she was moved to act as a floating battery. Unfortunately this success was not realised by the Allies. (IWM C4873)

by the RAF in late 1943, came into use on a regular basis with the Lancasters of No 3 Group from October 1944. Whereas Oboe worked by the transmissions of two ground stations interrogating apparatus in an aircraft, G-H worked the other way about, with an airborne device interrogating the two ground stations. The chief advantage lay in the fact that several aircraft could make use of G-H at the same time whereas Oboe had strict limitations. Although Oboe was considered more

precise, G-H proved to be accurate enough for effective 'blind bombing'.

The Americans also took up G-H for regular operational use. Having decided to pass Oboe to the B-26 Marauders of the Ninth Air Force, the Eighth established a B-24 squadron that began providing G-H leads in January 1944, mostly against V-weapon sites in the Pas de Calais. The Americans were so impressed with the results of G-H that one B-17 wing in the

Right: The 'boneyard' at Woodbridge emergency landing airfield, one of three with an extra long runway and laid out for the express purpose of homing damaged aircraft. Repair men in the foreground work on a Halifax wing. In the background, Lancaster LL624/JI:P of No 514 Squadron, one of the few squadrons to operate the radial-engine Mk II, will fly no more. Badly battle-damaged for the third time on a September 1944 raid, it was deemed beyond economical repair and struck off charge. Components were taken to make other Lancasters airworthy. (IWM CH21201)

Left, upper: Window cascades from the bay of No 101 Squadron's NG128/SR:C, piloted by W Off R. B. Tibbs, as it makes for Duisburg, 14 October 1944. The Airborne Cigar aerials are prominent above the fuselage. Few photographs of these special aircraft exist owing to the censor's work, but this view came from a motion picture, and eliminating the masts was not possible. (IWM CL1405)

Left, lower: The Aphrodite Project was a series of operational experiments with radio-controlled weapons. The technology was in its infancy, and little success was achieved. A major enterprise was taking old B-17s, stripping them of all armour, armament and other inessential equipment, fitting radio-control and loading 20,000lb of high explosive. To all intents and purposes a flying bomb, the aircraft was flown off conventionally and after setting the radio control the crew of two would bale out. The aircraft would then be guided by radio signals to a target, usually a substantial concrete structure for the protection of naval vessels. None of these strikes was successful. To aid the controller in the mother aircraft the drone was painted a bright yellow. That in the photograph (the aircraft at bottom right), heading for Heligoland and destruction on 15 October 1944, had, as a conventional B-17F bomber, flown many missions from Grafton Underwood before retirement. (USAAF)

Right: Another example of extraordinary damage to a returning bomber. As this aircraft, the 601st Bomb Squadron's 338172/3O:P, was approaching Cologne on 15 October 1944, an 88mm shell penetrated the nose. The denotation killed Sgt George Abbott, the togglier (the name for a non-rated bombardier who released bombs on seeing another aircraft's drop) and took away the whole upper nose section back to the cockpit windshield. Miraculously Lt Ray LeDoux, the navigator, though momentarily stunned, was not seriously wounded and was able to make his way back to the flight deck. Lt Lawrence De Lancey and his co-pilot, Lt Philip Stahlman, had to contend with an icy blast, failed instruments, no oxygen and no maps in bringing the bomber down to lower altitude and maintaining control all the way back to home base at Nuthampstead. (USAAF)

1st Division specialised in its use during the spring of 1944, providing pathfinder leads for other formations when requested. Some good results were obtained, even through conditions of complete undercast. Allied advances allowed new G-H stations to be placed on the continent. It was then that No 3 Group Lancasters commenced using G-H as their main aid in daylight attacks, copying the American practice of non-G-H equipped aircraft dropping on the sighted release from a G-H leader. As RAF formations were not as compact as those of the US bombers, it was usual to have one G-H Lancaster leading two without the equipment. No 3 Group's first major raid using G-H was on 18 October by four of 128 aircraft bombing Bonn, a virgin target city. From then on most G-H-led raids were against petroleum industry and communications targets in the Ruhr. In fact, No 3 Group averaged over three such raids a week until the end of the war.

Air Chief Marshal Harris still looked to the destruction of industrial cities to have the most telling effect in hastening the collapse of the enemy, a view he continued to expound but which was no longer met with such enthusiasm by his superior. Portal and other members of the Air Staff were aware that, with the new techniques and equipment, the strategic target objectives of the early war years were now attainable. The campaign against oil had already proved highly successful and Portal was in tune with Spaatz on this objective. The Air Ministry directive issued on 25 September clearly placed the petroleum industry as the main priority, and rail and water communications second with armoured and other military vehicle manufacturing. If Harris disagreed, in practice he had for some time cooperated with Spaatz by frequently sending a part of his force against oil and other targets that met the directive. Moreover, despite his disagreement with Portal he continued much in the same way. In January 1945 his bombers struck at more oil targets than the USAAF, although the latter's effort was on a reduced scale due to weather and support of ground forces. If RAF Bomber Command's effort against oil did not match the USAAF's in the number of raids or sorties, it more than matched it in destructive power, simply because of the much larger bombs employed.

Among the most useful of the big bombs was the 12,000lb Tallboy, a streamlined, deep-penetration missile first employed in June for precision tasks. Usually left to the specialised units on No 5 Group, Tallboys were employed in a successful breach of the Dortmund–Ems Canal on the night of 23/24 September, a target name that had been around since the early days of the war and was to be visited again.

Tallboys were also used in an attempt to prevent the Germans flooding certain areas to impede the advance of US ground forces—on 7 October against the lock gates of the Kembs dam, followed by five attempts between 4 and 11 December to breach the Roer dams although these were too robust to give. So was the Sorpe dam, one of the targets for the famous dams raid of May 1943 which Lancasters attacked with Tallboys on 15 October. This weapon was the eventual nemesis for the battleship *Tirpitz* in a Norwegian fjord when two direct hits from an attack by Lancasters on 12 November caused a crippling explosion and capsizing.

During the autumn and early winter RAF Bomber Command frequently despatched more than a thousand aircraft on a night's operations to several targets, and on 23/24 October 1,055 were sent to that prime Ruhr target Essen in semi-moonlight conditions. The light loss of five Lancasters and three Halifaxes was typical of this period of operations when compared with the heavy attrition that Ruhr targets had brought during the previous year. The ability to approach over liberated territory and shorten exposure to the Luftwaffe's defences was a major factor, although the night fighter force was in decline through personnel and fuel shortages plus the relentless pressure from the Allied air forces. Indeed, it was the Eighth Air Force, generally ranging further afield than RAF Bomber Command during this period, that usually sustained the heavier losses.

Spaatz pressed his oil campaign with 119 attacks by the Eighth and Fifteenth Air Forces during the last quarter of 1944, with a considerable weight still directed at tank and military vehicle production. The German raid reporting and control system was adept at identifying bomber formations devoid of

Above: This extraordinary photograph was taken within a second of a collision between two 305th Bomb Group B-17s flying over Thurleigh airfield. The formation was returning from an attack on the Hanomag armoured vehicle factory at Hanover on 22 October 1944 and, while visibility was not good, the reason for the two aircraft coming together is not known. There were no survivors among the nineteen crewmen. The large amount of air traffic over East Anglia made collisions almost inevitable in poor weather, and they averaged two a month. (USAAF)

Right: The reduction in RAF Bomber Command losses through expanding numbers and lessening enemy opposition saw a number of bombers reach the milestone of 100 sorties completed. One of the first Lancasters to achieve this was No 106 Squadron's command aircraft, frequently used by senior officers acting as the Master Bomber on operations. Named *King of the Air*, JB663/ZN:A was taken on charge at Metheringham in November 1943 and just under a year later, on 3/4 November 1944, it flew its hundredth raid. The NCO in charge of her ground crew was Flt Sgt A. V. Hallett, a boy entrant into the RAF with fifteen years' service. JB663 went on to complete at least another eleven sorties before being retired in February 1945. The photograph censor usually deleted the H2S radome under the rear fuselage, though not in this case. (IWM CH14239)

an escort and directing Luftwaffe fighters to the area. It was the *Sturmgruppen* with their heavily armed and armoured interceptors in mass assault that continued to be the most effective means of bringing down the B-17s and B-24s. Of 1,192 'heavies' sent out on 27 September, 28 were lost, two to flak and 26 B-24s to fighters. Of these 26, all but one were lost in a *Sturmgruppe* attack on a single group! The next day the same type of assault unit took eleven B-17s out of a formation. On 2 November, when 40 American 'heavies' were lost, thirteen were from fighter attack on a single group formation. That day the Luftwaffe fighters had a particularly hard time from the escorting Mustangs, which claimed over 100. The target was Merseburg, one of the most important synthetic oil production centres, ringed with what was probably the heaviest concentration of 88 and 105mm flak guns in the Reich. At least a dozen of the 'heavies' succumbed to their fire and several others sustained serious damage. For the American fliers Merseburg became the most infamous of targets with its ring of some 500 flak guns—no more so than after the mission of 30 November when an unforeseen strong headwind so slowed the bombers on their target approach that few escaped without some perforations and at first 56 were listed as missing. Many

Right: Not all the RAF 'heavies' in Italy were employed in a bombing role. No 148 Squadron's Halifaxes' main duty was supplying partisans in the Balkans, a task which was often more fraught with danger from the elements than from the enemy. The storm conditions over Albania and Yugoslavia were notorious, often frustrating these missions. Here aircrew at Brindisi load bundles for a sortie in LL385/FS:H, October 1944. When not employed on 'special duties', No 148 joined the other RAF night bombers in hauling more lethal cargoes. (IWM CNA3230)

damaged bombers had put down in liberated territory, but the final tally was 29 missing in action and twelve so badly damaged that they were beyond economical repair. Such was the speed of repair of the petroleum facilities that it was necessary to return again and again to the same target, and those in eastern Germany were the most heavily defended. At precisely 2045hrs on the evening of 6/7 December RAF Bomber Command made its first attack on the large Merseburg/Luna plant, delivering more destructive power with its larger bombs.

In mid-December 1944 a period of cold, foggy weather took hold in western Europe and remained stubbornly in place for many days. Expecting aircraft to be grounded on fog-shrouded airfields, von Rundstedt launched the last Wehrmacht ground offensive in the west, pushing out of the Ardennes in much the same way as he had done in 1940, with a similar intent of cutting Allied armies in two. After initial success the offensive was contained. For a week the Allied air forces were barred from giving much assistance by the weather. This began to

break on the 23rd and on Christmas Eve the Eighth Air Force and RAF Bomber Command airfields in East Anglia were able to launch attacks on communication targets that served the offensive base area. For the Eighth Air Force this was its greatest effort of the war, with the despatch of 2,046 B-17s and B-24s plus 853 escort fighters, bombing 25 primary targets, seven secondary targets and eighteen targets of opportunity. For two weeks the heavy bombers concentrated their power on communication targets and enemy airfields in a tactical role, which was becoming merged with strategic aims as the B-26 medium bombers, flying from French bases, were able to attack targets in Germany. Even so, Spaatz was soon able to send part of his force back to pounding the oil industry, with 526 B-17s briefed for seven installations in north-west Germany on the last day of the year. Once again, a short, sharp assault by Luftwaffe fighters took out a dozen B-17s from one group and five from another before the escort could arrive.

During January and February 1945 RAF Bomber Command put a greater tonnage of bombs on petroleum industry targets than the USAAF. On the night of 13/14 January its bombers produced the most devastating damage at Politz so far and at Merseburg/Leuna the next night, skilfully directed by the master bomber, caused destruction adjudged the most damaging of all attacks on this plant. After a further attack on Politz on 8/9 February the destruction was beyond repair and production ceased. To reduce interception by enemy fighters when attacking such northern targets, crews were briefed to overfly Sweden on their way back.

The Red Army's offensive in the east brought a request from the Soviets for heavy attacks on the major communication centres in the east to impede German reinforcements. Berlin, Chemnitz, Dresden, Magdeburg and others were identified, and the Allied planners thought that at this time such heavy bombardments might so affect morale that a collapse of the

Nazi regime would be hastened. It became a temporary secondary priority, but once again weather delayed the execution of this plan.

The Eighth Air Force staged the first major raid on Berlin for two months on 3 February, sending over a thousand bombers with marshalling yards as their primary targets. Weather again delayed further implementation until the night of 13/14 February, when Dresden was the target for 805 RAF bombers. The attack was extremely concentrated and caused fires akin to those that had burnt out the heart of Hamburg in 1943. The next day the Eighth Air Force arrived and added 771 US tons to the 2,660 tons dropped by the RAF, with the extensive railway installations as the aiming point. The Eighth Air Force returned the following day to dispense another 464 tons. The exact number of casualties was never established, but is generally held to be greater than at Hamburg, with estimates between 40,000 and 50,000. Chemnitz was also attacked by the Eighth Air Force on the 14th and by the RAF on that night, although bombing was scattered and the destruction far from the scale seen at Dresden. The high casualty reports increased unease in some quarters of the Allied commands, many questioning the need for such shattering blows when Germany was obviously near to defeat.

A period of fair weather, much as had occurred the previous year for the Big Week operations, allowed the USAAF to launch a massive and widespread assault on the German communication system, Operation Clarion, starting on 22 February. On that day 1,428 B-17s and B-24s were despatched to 25 targets, most hitherto untouched by aerial assault. Many were of relatively small area, and to ensure accuracy the 'heavies' reduced altitude to 10,000ft and in some cases, where clouds intervened, to considerably less. Next day 1,274 Eighth

Above: On 22/23 November 1944 Halifax JP321/V of No 614 Squadron, with Fg Off H. Weldon and crew, acted as 'illuminator' for a raid on the marshalling yards at Szombatheley, Hungary. At 2010hrs the Halifax was attacked twice in three minutes by a Ju 88 night fighter. The first enemy incendiaries set fire to two ammunition boxes in the rear fuselage, causing most of the rounds to detonate. Regardless of the hazard, the flight engineer, Sgt K. Briggs, extinguished the flames and the aircraft was brought back to its Amendola base in Italy without injury to the crew. (IWM CH17867)
Right: An external view of the damage to JP321. The aircraft was scrapped. (IWM CH17868)

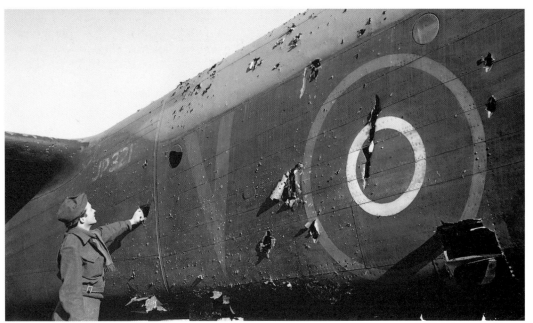

Air Force 'heavies' continued Clarion. Extensive damage was done through overall accurate bombing, with little seen of the Luftwaffe. Losses for the two days amounted to eight bombers missing.

Fighter interception was now very much the exception as both RAF Bomber Command and the Eighth Air Force regularly despatched over a thousand heavy bomber sorties in the improving spring weather. The Fifteenth Air Force, which had frequently to abandon missions into Germany and Austria during the winter because of appalling weather over the Alps, was also able to press attacks on communications and oil in the enemy's southern areas. Indeed, the weather conditions were so good that March 1945 saw the greatest tonnages of ordnance expended by the Allied air forces—153,541 by all USAAF forces in Europe and 91,901 by the RAF. Only occasionally could the Luftwaffe find the fuel to challenge. One of its successes was a concentrated intruder operation to catch RAF bombers over their bases on the night of 3/4 March.

Above: The liberation of much of France and Belgium allowed damaged and fuel-diminished bombers to put down on 2nd TAF- or Ninth Air Force-occupied airfields. Many Eighth Air Force 'heavies' put down on the RAF base at Brussels/Melsbroek, which had a US mobile repair unit as a lodger. When the Luftwaffe launched a mass strafing raid on Allied airfields on New Year's Day 1945, this airfield was among those to which considerable damage was done and where several bombers were destroyed. Here RAF firefighters attempt to douse the flames that burnt out the fuel tanks of the 391st Bomb Squadron's 338406/W. A smouldering B-24 wreck can be seen in the foreground. (R. Zorn) **Below, left and right:** The weather during the critical period of the Wehrmacht offensive through the Ardennes was particularly bad, with freezing fog and much snow. It contributed to several take-off crashes. On 1 January, when 850 bombers were despatched by the Eighth Air Force to attack communications targets through which von Runstedt's reinforcements would pass, five bombers crashed on take-off with the loss of 27 lives. The PFF leadplane of the 453rd Bomb Group formation, B-24J 251865/H6:H, piloted by Lt A. C. Judd, slid off the Old Buckenham runway, clipped two parked B-24s and was demolished against a hedgerow. Only two of the eleven men on board escaped with their lives. Two 447th Bomb Group B-17s were lost on take-off, but both crews escaped. B-17G 2102567/K, of the 709th Bomb Squadron, caught fire and the bomb load blew up, scattering debris around a frozen ploughed field. The tailwheel lies forlornly in the foreground of the photograph, and base personnel can be seen inspecting the wreckage on the far side of the field. There was not one Eighth Air Force bomber base that did not experience a take-off crash at some time during its operational use; at most there were more than one. (USAAF)

Nearly 100 night fighters were reported to have been involved, shooting down thirteen Halifaxes, five Lancasters, a Fortress and a Mosquito. They also strafed 27 British and American airfields, in the course of which three of the intruders were lost.

To aid the Russians RAF Bomber Command attacked Chemnitz on 5/6 March and Nuremberg on the 16th/17th. The Eighth Air Force sent 1,329 'heavies' to Berlin on 18 March, its largest number against a single target city, and a few of the thirteen lost fell to one of the strongest interceptions by Me 262 jets. The Fifteenth Air Force made its only attack on Berlin six days later, sending 150 B-17s on the thousand-mile round trip from its Italian bases. Berlin had had little peace throughout the winter, for No 8 Group Mosquitos raided regularly. With eleven squadrons and some 200 Mosquitos, raids of 50 to 70 on a single target were not uncommon, the aircraft's speed making night fighter interception rare. The 200 to 240 tons dropped nightly would once have been considered a sizeable attack. From 20/21 February Mosquitos kept up visits to Berlin for 36 nights in succession. In terms of numbers, RAF Bomber Command's largest raid against a single target was the 1,108 sent to Dortmund in daylight on 12 March 1945, when 4,851 tons were unloaded through cloud on radar aim.

Aware that their largest bombs had little effect on the enormous concrete structures the Germans had built to protect U-

Right, top: Sometimes the flak was accurate, sometimes it was not. The flak gunners had it just right on 13 January 1945 when the 303rd Bomb Group was given a rail bridge at Mannheim to destroy. The weather was clear and cold and the radar prediction was precise, for the flak salvos brought down three, severely damaged fourteen and caused minor damage to seven of the 38 B-17s involved. The losses were all from the 427th Bomb Squadron formation. 2/Lt O. T. Eisenhart's 338689/GN:A took a direct hit in the tail and plummeted earthwards. No one escaped, probably held by the gravitational forces of the rapid descent. The leadplane of a higher squadron caught the plunge with its strike camera. Over 900 bombers were out that day and only four others were lost. (USAAF)

Right, centre: RAF Bomber Command made more raids on Essen than on any other city in Germany, laying waste an estimated 50 per cent of this major site of Ruhr industry. The 28th and last main force raid was made in daylight on 11 March 1945, 1,079 aircraft being involved, the second largest total ever sent out by Bomber Command to a single target. As a complete undercast

veiled Essen, Oboe marking was used. Extensive cloud can be seen in this photograph of a Lancaster discharging Window to disrupt gunlaying radar images. Window was in 216 packs of 2,200 metallised strips each measuring approximately 25cm ∞ 2cm. Bundles took 20 to 30 seconds to disperse sufficiently to be effective and could disrupt enemy radar for up to 20 minutes, depending on the height from which they were dropped. The descent rate was 300–400ft per minute, varying according to the dozen or so different types of Window discharged. (IWM C5634)

Right, bottom: Fires in Dresden on the night of 13/14 February 1945. (IWM C4971)

boat and E-boat pens and V-weapons stores, the British developed a massive 22,000lb missile known as Grand Slam. On 14 March the special task Lancaster unit attacked viaducts near the Ruhr with this weapon and succeeded in bringing down that at Bielefeld which had defied the 2,000lb bombs of several Eighth Air Force attacks. On the same day another British missile, the 7,000lb Disney rocket bomb, was successfully employed by Eighth Air Force B-17s against E-boat pens at Ijmuiden. These concrete penetrating missiles, unsuitable for carriage in the bays of British bombers, were delivered via underwing racks on Eighth Air Force Fortresses.

By mid-April the Allied armies had overrun much of Germany and few targets of a strategic nature remained for the heavy bombers. Communications and enemy airfields received most attention, and opposition was often non-existent. One exception was an Eighth Air Force mission to airfields and marshalling yards in central Germany, when five B-17s were brought down by deliberate ramming by Luftwaffe fighters, the only occasion when such a tactic was known to have occurred.

The last Eighth Air Force heavy bomber raid was to targets in the Pilsen and Salzburg areas on 25 April. A broadcast prior to the raid to warn Czech workers of the impending attack alerted the flak defences, resulting in six B-17s being shot down.

RAF Bomber Command attacked an oil storage depot in Norway that night and then, with the Eighth Air Force, delivered food to starving Dutch civilians in the areas of Holland still held by the Germans. The last RAF Bomber Command raid was against Kiel on the night of 2/3 May 1945, the object being to prevent the escape of shipping. The two Halifaxes lost were believed to have collided.

Left, upper: By late 1944 No 205 Group RAF in Italy had come to standardise on the Liberator for heavy bomber operations, eventually having six squadrons and some 120 aircraft. Airfield conditions in Italy were far from good, ranging from the blinding dust of high summer to snow and slush in winter. The latter were much in evidence at Foggia in January 1945. (IWM CNA3370)
Left, lower: PA995/BQ:V, *The Vuture Strikes*, was the third Lancaster of No 550 Squadron to complete 100 raids, reaching the century on 5/6 March 1945 with Fg Off G. Blackler and crew, Blackler finishing his own tour on this night. All those in the squadron associated with this aircraft posed for a commemorative picture. Included are the CO, Wg Cdr J. C. MacWatters, two WAAFs, the padre and the inevitable dog mascot. George Blackler is in the cockpit. Such a record was no insurance for continued longevity, for this bomber failed to return from its next operation with another crew on 7/8 March to Dessau. (IWM CH14853)
Right: Col Henry Terry, CO of the 91st Bomb Group, congratulates mission leader Lt Col Immanuel Klette on a job well done, the destruction of a rail bridge at Vlotho, 14 March 1945. Both were veterans of the Eighth Air Force's early days, Henry Terry having come to England with the 306th Bomb Group in 1942. 'Manny' Klette began his combat career in the same group in March 1943 and, despite serious injury in a flying accident, persisted in flying missions. He led the 91st on the last mission of the war, his 91st combat sortie and a record unsurpassed by any other Eighth Air Force bomber pilot. (USAAF)

Left, top: The once proud *Tirpitz*, now capsized, photographed by a low-level reconnaissance Mosquito in Tromsø Fjord on 22 March 1945. Salvage vessels are in attendance, but from the little snow that has been removed it appears that no major salvage operation is in progress. It was on 12 November 1944 that a force of 38 Lancasters dropping 28 Tallboys had secured at least two direct hits. That same day, photographic evidence that the *Tirpitz* had turned over was obtained. (IWM C5148A)

Left, centre: Wg Cdr J.B. 'Tirpitz' Tate, DSO and Bar, DFC, who replaced Leonard Cheshire as CO of No 617 Squadron, photographed with his crew. The Lancaster, EE146/KC:D, is the aircraft Tate flew on both raids on the *Tirpitz*; it had both dorsal and nose turrets removed, in order to reduce weight and improve handling with Tallboy bombs. A replacement for the dams raid losses in June 1943, this Lancaster served No 617 until badly damaged on 6 April 1945. (IWM CH178764)

Left, bottom: The Arbergen rail bridge over the River Weser was destroyed by a 'Ten Ton Bomb' on 21 March 1945 when No 617 Squadron paid a visit. The Lancaster, which appears to be PB996/YZ:C, flown by Sqn Ldr Calder, is a Mk I Special without nose or dorsal armament. (IWM C5102)

Right, top and centre: The Bielefeld viaduct had survived several attempts at severance by the Eighth Air Force, whose 2,000lb bombs proved to have insufficient power to demolish the structure effectively. On 14 March 1945 No 617 Squadron attacked with fourteen 12,000lb Tallboys and the first 22,000lb Grand Slam, delivered by Sqn Ldr C. C. Calder's crew. The first photograph was taken before the raid on 5 March and the second three days after the attack. Two parallel viaducts were demolished or distorted over a hundred yards' length, a third of the overall length of the structure. (IWM C5085/C5086)

Right, bottom: Struck by two bombs from a higher Liberator, Sqn Ldr L. C. Saxby and crew in KK320/V of No 37 Squadron had a miraculous escape. One bomb struck the port inner engine and sheared off the propeller and the second went through the fuselage just behind the flight deck, narrowly missing the top-turret gunner, P Off Walter Lewis. Lewis later described the incident: 'I was looking up and saw a bomb leave an aircraft above us. I saw it getting bigger and bigger as it came towards us. The next thing I realised was that the fuselage had been hit near the flight deck and I seemed to be pushed down in front of my seat. The perspex above me was taken clean off. All that happened to me was a bump on the shoulder.' Despite the damage, Saxby managed to regain control and fly the aircraft the near-300 miles back to home station at Tortorella. The target was Monfalcone port and the date 16 March 1945. (IWM C5163)

Left, upper: In the final days of the war the strategic bombers were running out of targets as the advancing land forces reduced the enemy's stronghold. To prevent the enemy's use of his airfields and to damage as many aircraft thereon as possible, both Eighth and Fifteenth Air Forces flew several missions in April 1945 to disseminate fragmentation bombs on these sites. Here 460th Bomb Group Liberators are making a drop over an airfield in Austria. The 20lb M-41s were loaded in clusters of either six or twenty-five, which released immediately after leaving the bomb bay; the freed cluster bands can be seen in this photograph. Unlike the Eighth Air Force aircraft, these Fifteenth Air Force B-24s have retained their ball turrets. (USAAF)

Left, lower: It was policy, where possible, to assign individuals from a Commonwealth country to one of the squadrons having a named association with that country. No 44 Squadron was associated with Rhodesia and many of its airmen were Rhodesians. If the cost of an aircraft or some item of equipment was specifically subscribed for 'their' squadron, this was usually acknowledged with a suitable inscription and presentation photograph. The employees of Shabani Mines in Southern Rhodesia contributed £1,255, and this was used for a petrol bowser. On hand for the photograph were Fg Off Plenderleith, aged 21 and with 34 sorties to his credit; Flt Sgt Van Niekerk, aged 19 with 26 sorties; and Cpl Simpson, a fitter; all the men were from Shabani. *Sky Floosie* is LM625/KM:H with 78 raid symbols, those for daylight sorties painted white. (IWM CH15011)

Right, upper: The biggest totals of sorties completed were run up by the speedy Mosquitos of No 8 Group. The Oboe units, Nos 105 and 109 Squadrons, had several aircraft with more than a hundred sorties. Mosquito LR503/GB:<u>F</u>, seen here at Bourn with 203 trips marked up, went on to complete another ten. It was usual for the transparent nosepiece to be painted over on Oboe-equipped Mosquitoes. (IWM CH15099)

Right, lower: Fewer Halifaxes reached the century mark than Lancasters, partly because there were fewer of them in Bomber Command—some 500 compared with 1,300 Lancasters by early spring 1945. LV937/MH:E *Expensive Babe*, of No 51 Squadron, was one centurion, reaching this mark on the Osnabrück raid of 25 March 1945. Gp Cpt B. D. Sellick DFC, the station commander at Snaith, was there to greet the crew on their return. They are Flt Lt R. Kemp, pilot; Flt Sgt A .C. Townsend, navigator; Flt Sgt J. D. Silberberg, air bomber; W Off R. J. Williams, wireless operator; Sgt E. S. Hawkins, flight engineer; Flt Sgt R. T. Jackson, air gunner; and Flt Sgt F. Thwaites, air gunner. Townsend and Silberberg were Australians and Hawkins a New Zealander—making another Bomber Command crew composed of mixed nationalities. LV937 had started out with No 578 Squadron in March 1944, with which it served for only a month. The swastika symbol is for a Ju 88 claim. (IWM CH15163)

Far left, upper: A Grand Slam loaded on a Lancaster B.I Special, PD113/YZ:T, at Woodhall Spa prior to delivery to the Farge pens, 27 March 1945. The crew are Fg Off E. W. Weaver, air bomber; Fg Off R. P. Barry, rear gunner; Flt Lt. J. L. Sayer DFC, pilot; Fg Off V. L. Johnson, flight engineer; and Fg Off F. E. Wittmer, navigator. Towards the end of hostilities Bomber Command had an increasing number of all-officer crews. Lancasters dropped a total of 41 Grand Slams operationally. (IWM MH15076)

Far left, lower: The Eighth Air Force was sent to Dresden again on 17 April 1945, specifically to attack the railyards to aid the Russian advance. This is the strike as recorded by the leadplane of the 91st Bomb Group, B-17G 338088/LG:R, *Red Wing*, from 21,000ft. Two aiming points show up, with contentrations of bomb bursts on and adjacent to each. Me 262 jets attacked the 91st Group, causing damage but no losses. (USAAF)

Left: The Grand Slam achieved what other free-fall bombs had failed to do—penetrate the tremendously thick concrete shelters that protected E-boat and U-boat construction and harbouring. Carrying Grand Slams, No 617 Squadron visited the Valentin submarine works at Farge, near Bremen, on 27 March 1945. Photo-reconnaissance had covered the construction of the protective buildings at Farge since November 1943 and the work was nearing completion when twelve of the 22,000lb missiles descended. Two made direct hits and penetrated the seven metres of reinforced concrete. (IWM CL2606)

Below: The Fortress and Liberator were slow old ladies by the spring of 1945, when a frequent antagonist was the Me 262 twin-jet fighter. Fortunately the 300–400mph approach speed of the Me 262 was usually too fast for accurate sighting on the lumbering 180mph bombers. When a 5.5cm R4M rocket projectile from an Me 262 did hit home, the damage was considerable. Lucky were Lt Shaffer and the crew of the 600th Bomb Squadron's 48699/N8:Q on 10 April 1945 when seeking to bomb airfields in the Oranienburg area from which it was believed the jets were operating. They made Manston safely. Unlike the Allied air forces which soldiered on to the end with the same weapon types, the Germans developed guns and other armament specifically for air fighting. (USAAF)

Above: When Allied troops entered Düsseldorf in April 1945 they found the remains of a Halifax lodged against the wall of the city's municipal offices. It appears to have been ZA:V of No 10 Squadron. (IWM CL2444)

Below: Unfinished U-boats in a Hamburg shipyard on 3 May 1945. Production was pursued despite the repeated bombing of Germany's second largest city, but only with great difficulty in the final months of hostilities. (IWM CL2502)

9
THE RECKONING

Air power was indisputably a decisive factor in the Allied victory, if the contribution of the RAF and USAAF strategic bombing offensive is less clear. The first two years of RAF Bomber Command activities can have had little effect upon the German war economy and were probably no more than a dangerous nuisance. With the expansion that began in 1942 and displays of strength such as the 'Thousand Plan' raids, night attacks became a serious threat. The Combined Bomber Offensive of 1943 and early 1944 by the RAF and USAAF caused considerable disruption to war production, yet German industry still managed to increase the output

Below: Instead of bombs, the bays of No 3 Group Lancasters were filled with food parcels during the first days of May 1945. These were delivered to the starving Dutch population in those areas where German forces had been bypassed by the Allied advances. *Edith*, LM577/HA:Q, got its name with No 622 Squadron, who operated the Lancaster for some five months. No 218 Squadron received the aircraft after depot maintenance and by 28 April 1945 had raised the sortie total to 84. When this photograph was taken at Chedburgh, *Edith* had

also flown fourteen food-dropping and POW-collection sorties, and had more hours' flying time on it than any other Lancaster in the squadron. The Lancaster in the background bearing the codes XH:D is a 'C' Flight aircraft. Several No 3 Group Squadrons added a third flight, taking their aircraft establishments to more than 30. The alphabet having been outrun, an additional squadron code was bestowed in order to obtain individual identities. (IWM CH15460)

of the main fighting machines. The number of armoured fighting vehicles turned out per month was double that of two years previously by the date of the Normandy invasion, while, despite its being a main objective, aircraft production rose from some 25,000 in 1943 to more than 39,000 in 1944. Not until the latter half of that year, when the British and American strategic air forces had finally achieved planned strengths, was truly telling destruction wrought on the German war economy, chiefly through the depredation of the oil installations and the extensive railway system. The tanks and fighter aircraft were still being made, if at a severely reduced rate, but there was little fuel to power them or means to deliver them to the armed services.

Beyond this, during the final months of the war Allied air power was so great that a wide range of target systems were attacked, compounding the difficulties of the Third Reich and hastening its collapse. Strategic bombing never achieved the ideals of some of its promoters—that it alone could decide the outcome of a conflict by bringing about the complete breakdown of the enemy's war economy, thus avoiding the need to defeat his armies in the field. The great force necessary to meet this aim was not available until the last year of hostilities and was then frequently diverted to war contingencies, mostly in support of the ground forces. In these last months strategic bombing was certainly going some way towards achieving its original objectives, inasmuch as from the autumn of 1944 there

was a rapid fall-off in most types of military production in Germany.

Apart from its destructive might, the bomber offensive imposed a tremendous strain on the Reich infrastructure through defence, dispersal, repair and rehabilitation, involving an estimated two million persons. The priority production of fighter aircraft and flak weapons took resources that might otherwise have been directed to providing for ground or sea forces. The dispersal of vulnerable manufacturing industry contributed to lost production and added to the pressures on transportation. The repair of bombed buildings and factory facilities required a vast labour force, although this could be met by foreign and 'slave' workers drawn from the Nazi empire. The re-housing of thousands of bombed-out civilians was another not inconsiderable strain.

During the Second World War approximately four million tons of bombs were used by the British and American air forces against Germany and her allies. There are differing figures in official records for the composition of this tonnage, as with most other statistics relating to the strategic bombing offensive, and the following may be considered arbitary. The US Eighth Air Force expended 692,918 tons, the US Fifteenth Air Force 312,173 tons and RAF Bomber Command 955,044 tons. The percentage distribution of these tonnages against the strategic objective targets by the commands mentioned is as follows:

Type of target	USAAF	RAF
Petroleum and oil	13.1	10.2
Communications	26.7	14.4
Industrial towns	0.7	45.1
German Air Force	9.8	2.7
Military installations	8.6	6.8
Naval	1.7	4.9
Specific industries	3.8	2.1
Army support	35.6	12.8
Miscellaneous	–	1.0

(Petroleum includes storage, synthetic oil and associated plants. Communications covers rail, road and water transport systems. German Air Force = aircraft and aero-engine factories, depots and airfields. Military installations = V-weapon sites, storage depots etc. Specific industries = rubber, chemcials, tanks, vehicles, bearings etc. Army support = tactical missions against troop concentrations, defensive positions etc.)

The RAF area bombing was chiefly against industrial cities, their war industries and transportation centres. As related, so-called area bombing came about primarily because Bomber Command was incapable of carrying out precision attacks in darkness. Heavy bombing of a city would kill or render homeless the workers who staffed the war factories in addition to destroying electricity, water, and other supporting facilities. Civilians were going to be killed and maimed, but in the light of German bombing of British cities there was little sympathy for the enemy citizen. Although the USAAF, with few exceptions, selected industrial or military targets for precision attack, some bombing was often astray and resulted in civilian casualties in the neighbourhood of the target. When cloud obstructed, as it often did, bombing by ground-scanning radar amounted to area bombing, although the developments in technique gradually brought more accuracy into such attacks. By the standards of later years, the precision bombing of the Second World War was a very imprecise science.

Breaking the enemy's morale by heavy bombing was an objective of some in the the RAF hierarchy although few, if any, believed this tenable by the final months of the offensive. Undoubtedly human morale will fail under prolonged horrific experience and there were instances when this did appear to be happening to the population of some war-torn cities. However, the destruction of a city is not the destruction of a nation. Like the citizens of London, the citizens of Berlin and other German urban conurbations showed remarkable resilience; in short, people come to terms with adversity of this kind.

The will of the German peoples had been immeasurably strengthened by the pronouncement and reiteration of Churchill and Roosevelt at the Casablanca Conference, early in 1943, that the Allies would accept nothing short of 'unconditional surrender'. Hitherto the German peoples had the idea that the Allies were fighting, as their propaganda proclaimed, Nazi Germany, whereas the declaration portended the knell of doom to the German nation as a whole if the Allies won. This grave political error was taken without full consultation with the military leaders. Much was made of this by Nazi propaganda and was further fuelled later in the war by the release of the Merganthan plan for the de-industrialisation of Germany. It left the German people with no hope except to hold out until the promised V-weapons would turn the tide of battle. Nevertheless, a loss of national morale was evident during the final months of the war among a people facing defeat and aided the Allied victory; but then it came from the cumulative effect of all Germany's woes.

Perhaps the most significant contribution of the strategic bombing offensive was a development neither planned or foreseen in the early days—the achievement of air superiority in enemy skies. This came about through the USAAF's need to protect its day bombers through developing long-range fighter escort. Through the winter of 1943–44, but primarily in the early spring of the latter year, American long-range fighters caused the demise of the Luftwaffe through both aerial combat and attacks on airfields. This not only allowed the bombers to go about their work with lower attrition but gave the Allies domination of the air over the battle fronts following the invasion of the continent. Ironically, the principal fighter type involved, the P-51 Mustang, was originally ordered and built for the RAF, whose leadership initially discounted the belief that a single-engine, long-range fighter could hold its own with the best of its adversaries. This no doubt resulted from the experiences of the early war years when the interceptor fighter was seen as paramount. RAF Bomber Command had chosen to further its operations under cover of darkness in order to minimise the chances of fighter interception. Unfortunately, that same darkness hid the night fighter which, with radar aids, came to make the night bomber's chances of survival much less than that of the day bomber. There was no escort to deal with the Luftwaffe night fighters.

The advocacy of the self-defending heavy bomber in prewar planning was never matched with efforts to give this substance by its promoters. There was little hope of a large aircraft, defended by rifle-calibre weapons, enduring against a fighter with cannon. The RAF bombers were usually outranged by the heavy armament of the German night fighters and an effort to lessen this disadvantage was brought about through the enterprise of one of the combat organisations, which enlisted the services of a local firm to install the heavier .50-calibre machine guns in rear turrets. The USAAF appreciated the advantage of this weapon, which had much better range and greater destructive power than the rifle-calibre machine guns, making it standard for bomber defence. Even so, this was no match for cannon fire. Neither the British nor the Americans developed and introduced cannon or machine guns specifically for air fighting, in contrast to the Germans, who developed several types. RAF Bomber Command lost 8,655 aircraft in the course of the war while engaged in operations plus some 1,600 through accident and write-offs. The Eighth and Fifteenth Air Forces lost 9,466 aircraft to all causes.

The cost in German lives as a result of the British and American strategic bomber offensive has been put at some 300,000 dead and 800,000 injured. Total casualty figures for RAF Bomber Command amounted to near 74,000, of whom 55,750 were killed in combat and accident. The USAAF never produced precise figures for the various air forces or separated these from the total casualties of more than 91,000, which figure includes prisoners of war. However, the combined Eighth and Fifteenth Air Force dead was approximately 30,000—a lower total relative to aircraft losses than the RAF, reflecting

the greater number of aircrew who were able to parachute to safety. Escape from an RAF 'heavy' was more difficult. The total British and American aircrew killed and wounded during the strategic bombing offensive amount to over 100,000. Only the German U-boat crews suffered a higher percentage loss of their personnel.

Much has been written of the loss of life and disablement suffered by bomber crews and some commentators have ventured to suggest that much of it was an unnecessary sacrifice. But no one can accurately assess what greater loss of life there might have been had not Germany been weakened by industrial destruction, transportation disruption and diversion of manpower by the bombing campaign. Had that not been so, the invasion of the continent in 1944 might not have succeeded, with all that would have meant to the peoples of occupied countries. Or, if it had been launched, against a greatly stronger enemy, then we have the horrendous casualties of the First World War to show what can result from evenly matched ground forces. Moreover, the more prolonged the conflict the greater was the threat of Germany producing and using a decisive weapon. The war aims were to bring the war to its earliest possible conclusion, and in that the strategic bombing campaign played a major part.

Below: Strictly against regulations, but a blind eye was turned by the authorities to the discharge of brightly coloured signal flares on the night of 8 May 1945. The war in Europe was over. The silhouetted B-17 and the sixty others on the field at Eye had suddenly become obsolete weapons, as had many hundreds of other British and American bombers in Europe. They were now part of history. (A. N. Delmonico)